HISTORY IN FOCUS

Looking at Houses

Audrey Gee

Batsford Academic and Educational Ltd London

Typeset by Tek-Art Ltd, London SE20
and printed in Great Britain by
R.J. Acford
Chichester, Sussex
for the publishers
Batsford Academic and Educational Ltd,
an imprint of B.T. Batsford Ltd,
4 Fitzhardinge Street
London W1H 0AH

ISBN 0 7134 0845 6

To Jeremy, my architect nephew

ACKNOWLEDGMENT

The Author and Publishers would like to
thank Betty Peakin, for all the drawings in
the book (figures 1-104); Richard Tames for
photographs 105, 106, 107, 108, 111, 112,
117; and Terry Williams for photographs
110, 113, 114, 115, 116, 118, 119, 120.
Figure 109 is by the Author.

Contents

Foreword

Looking at the separate parts of a house is less demanding than looking at the whole building, and often far more interesting. There is a story to be told about every feature — the walls, the roof, the door, the windows, the chimneys, inside. You can learn to judge how each feature fits into the evolution of the house as you see it today. Eventually, however, knowledge of the separate features will help you to look at the whole building with better understanding and to recognize its place in a street and in the ever-changing community.

The exploration of local influences makes the study of houses fascinating. Every area has its own local building materials, which give the houses there a characteristic colour and style. Even when transport became mechanized, the cost of transporting heavy stone was so great that many regional differences were maintained. Thus, while Welsh slate was as popular in Victorian London as in its place of origin, pink Devon granite houses are rare in Kent, as are flint cottages in Aberdeen. Garden rockeries and cemeteries, on the other hand, have a different tale to tell the geologist. Local builders and their architects have also given the houses in their area a particular character.

This book gives background information on the development of the main features of the home, but there are many other smaller features that can be investigated, such as front door "furniture", and collections can be made of objects or photographs taken that are of personal interest.

Once you start to look at houses, with an enquiring, comparing eye, the routine walk past familiar buildings becomes a quest, concerning the past, present and future. Concentrate on a feature that appeals to you and use this book like an encyclopaedia; look up the chapter relevant to your feature and bring it to life with your investigation results.

1
Walls

"What is it made of?" To answer this question about a house you will probably look first of all at the walls. It is a fairly easy question to answer if the walls are of plain brick or stone, though even brick and stone walls can be deceiving in eighteenth-century houses — a tile hanging, to give a wall the appearance of brick, and stone cladding were fashionable eighteenth-century devices. Walls covered in plaster, hanging tiles or weather-board all require further investigation if you want to discover the basic building material.

Britain can be roughly divided into two main geological areas when local building materials are discussed. A line from Devon to Yorkshire can be drawn to divide the lowlands of sedimentary deposits from the highlands of old, igneous and metamorphic rocks. In the lowland areas, where hardwood trees grew well, timber or mud and thatch were used for early homes, replaced later by brick and tile. In the highland areas, local stone was used for better homes and public buildings such as the local church, and so the towns and villages took on the stone colour of the area. Poorer homes used timber frames with rubble and plaster infilling and thatch roofs.

Lowland homes show the greater diversity in building materials, because the original materials deteriorated readily, in spite of the different wall claddings which were used. Technical improvement in brick and tile making revolutionized the building of ordinary homes. In the highland areas, where stone is the dominant material, it is changes in secondary features rather than in wall materials that are noticeable. During the present century, however, brick and cement tiles have become universal building materials.

1   The distribution of building materials.
▼

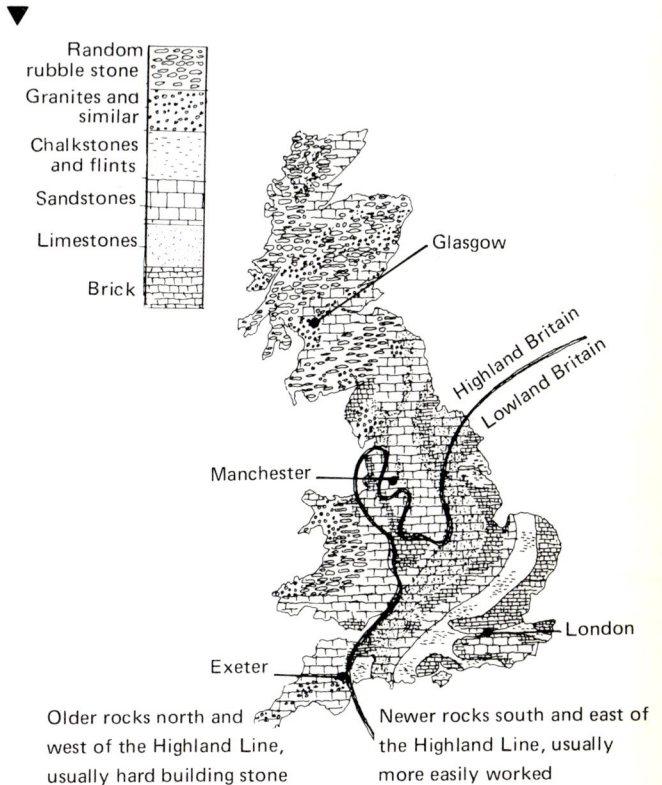

Older rocks north and west of the Highland Line, usually hard building stone

Newer rocks south and east of the Highland Line, usually more easily worked

5

The simplest house to build is the one that uses the materials found on the chosen site. A thousand years ago wood and mud were plentiful and so these materials were used to build the family homes.

In Devon, houses can still be seen made of *cob*. Cob is a mud made by mixing well together soil, clay, straw and gravel. Layers of the mixture were laid on a stone base, to build the walls of the house. Each layer, or *course*, was covered in straw and left to dry before the next layer was put on top. Building a cob wall therefore took some time, depending on the weather, but needed little building skill. Holes were cut out with a sharp blade for doors and windows, when the cob was partly dry. This avoided the need for a *lintel*, a supporting beam over doors or windows. The house was then given a thatched roof which overhung the walls to give them protection. The walls were also coated with a lime plaster which was tarred or whitewashed when dry.

In Buckinghamshire houses were made in a similar way, but the mud mixture contained a high proportion of chalk and was called "*whychert*".

The East Anglian equivalent of the cob house is the *clay lump* house. The walls were made of large clay and straw bricks, that were formed in moulds and left to dry naturally for several weeks. These large, unfired clay lumps were laid in *courses* or rows on a low stone or flint wall and were *mortared* or joined with a finer clay mixture. The finished wall could be tarred, to prevent farm animals licking the walls, but for a better appearance the tarred walls could be sanded while wet, then limewashed. Lime plaster *rendering* was an alternative to tarring and this was often colour-washed in pink, blue or green when dry. Since the seventeenth century East Anglia has also been famous for decorating its plastered walls with indented and moulded patterns. These are made on wet plaster and are called *pargetting*.

▲
2   A Devon cob house.

When gravel, stone chippings or coarse sand were added to lime plaster, this gave the walls a textured appearance and this *roughcast* was another common rendering for unbaked earth walls. In Scotland roughcast was used on stone walls to give the building an even colour, which was considered desirable, and here it was called *harling*.

3   Pargetting.
▼

Timber-Framed Walls

Examples of timber-framed houses built in medieval and Tudor times can still be found, although some are not immediately obvious as the walls may have been completely plastered over, partly covered by weatherboard or tile-hung. These wall coverings became popular from the late seventeenth century, to give protection from weathering and fire hazards.

The Saxon *cruck house* is one kind of timber-framed house, examples of which can be found notably in Herefordshire. These houses were built by setting apart on the ground two tree trunks, which were then bent over to meet overhead, to form a triangle. This was called the *cruck*. Another cruck was set about five metres away and the space between was known as a *bay*. The crucks were joined at the top, and vertical posts formed the lower walls. The frame of the building then looked like an upturned boat. The spaces between the posts were called *pans* and were infilled to make the solid house wall, or a pan could be left to make a doorway or window. The infilling in the earliest days was with split laths of wood, but later with woven twigs when wood became scarce, and this formed the *wattle* which was covered with *daub*, a mixture of mud, straw and dung. When the daub had hardened, it was plastered with a lime and cowhair mixture and this in turn was whitewashed or colour-washed. Three bays length seems to have been the average size for a house, although more crucks could be added for larger buildings.

The *box-framed* timber house superseded the cruck frame by the Tudor period. As the name suggests, it was built, like a log cabin, in a cuboid shape, rather than in the triangular shape of the Saxon cruck house. The box frame made it possible to have upper rooms, and town houses were built several storeys high. Carpentry skills were needed to build a box-frame which was constructed on the ground, often some distance from the site on which the house was to be erected —

4   A cruck gable house.

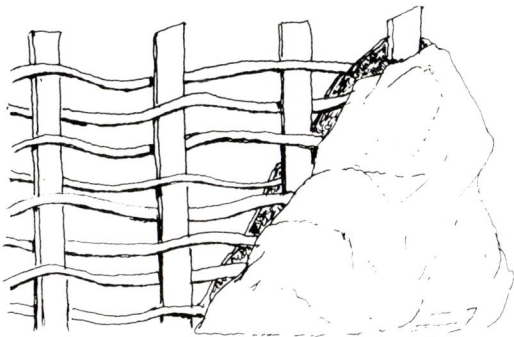

5   Wattle and daub.

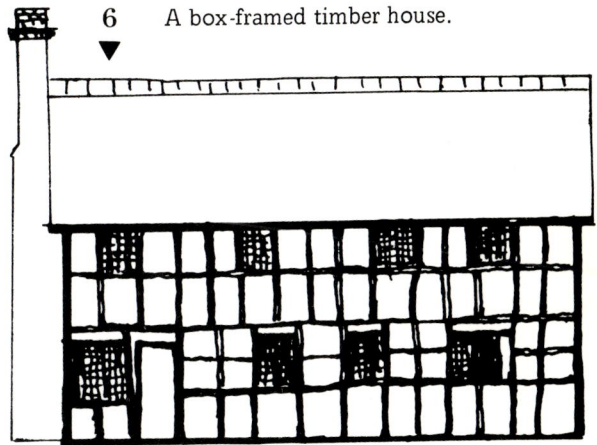

6   A box-framed timber house.

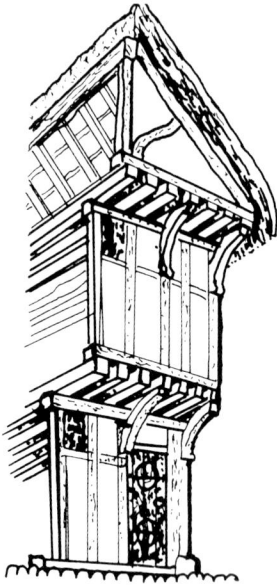

7   A jetty house.

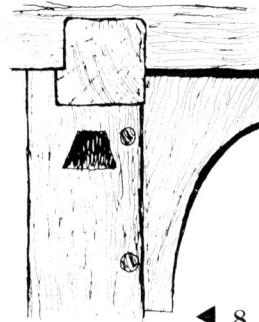

◀ 8   Wooden pegs and joints.

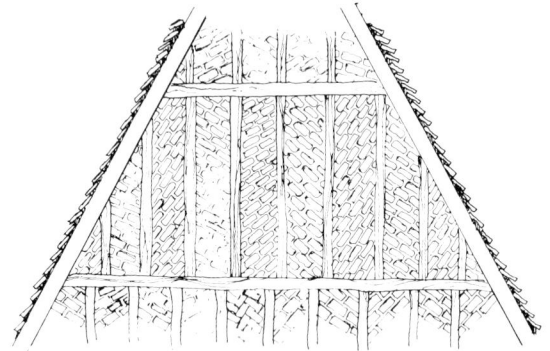

9   Herringbone nogging.

an early version of prefabrication. To aid assembly, carpenters made marks on the timber and these can still be seen on some roof beams. Wooden pegs were used to join the timbers, as nails were not used as freely as today. Nails were hand-made by a blacksmith on an anvil, if they were large, or in a *die* (a mould), if they were small. Hand-made nails can be recognized by their shape: they are not tubular as modern machine-made nails are, but square-shaped lengths in variable sizes as we have today. When the box-frame was ready, it was erected on a stone foundation or a base of beaten earth, which provided an even site for the building. The pans between the posts were infilled with wattle and daub — nails being used to secure the laths or woven twigs to the posts before the daub was applied. This was white-washed when dry. The distance between the posts varied according to the supply of timber, but in the late Tudor period, when timber was scarce, the pans were wide.

When houses were built several storeys high, especially in towns, the upper floors overhung the street, forming *jetties*. The upper rooms thus had more space and the jetties protected the walls below from the rain — drain pipes and gutters, as we know them, were not in general use in this period. The town house jetty also served as a canopy for the shop fronts below on the street, protecting goods on display. When bricks became cheaper, from the seventeenth century onwards, it became popular to repair the plastered wattle and daub walls by infilling with brick, and this was called *nogging*.

Stone Walls

Stone is an ideal building material if it is available locally. Although it is subject to some weathering, it makes a strong, dry, fireproof home. The highland zone of Britain favours stone building.

In the lowlands it was the Fire of London in 1666 which heralded the era of stone and brick homes. An Act of Parliament in 1667 required that all new homes in the city of London should be built of brick or stone and should have solid *party walls* — walls shared by two homes. This Rebuilding Act laid down the four types of house that were to be built. Side streets and lanes were to contain two-storey houses with an attic and cellar; three-storey houses were to be situated on major streets; four-storey houses were to be built on main roads; and the merchant's mansion, no higher than four storeys, could be built set back along main streets. The width of lanes was to be about five metres and of major roads eight to ten metres and it was hoped that roads of these sizes would form fire-breaks in the future. Gutters with downpipes were also made compulsory, which made the pedestrian's life more pleasant, for until this act rain water was channelled into spouts directly off the roof, and fell straight into the street. Town planning had arrived to bring order into the haphazard rapid growth of Tudor and Stuart towns, which had led to the disastrous Fire of 1666. In the next few years successive acts regulated the use of timber and its exposure, the thickness of walls and the building of chimney-stacks — all aimed at fire prevention. Building regulations at national and local level are still being added to and are a study in themselves!

Stone is a relatively expensive building material, even in a local situation, for it has to be cut or blasted from quarries and then transported to the building site. Transporting stone was laborious and difficult even over short distances before the transport revolution of the nineteenth century. In the early days stone quarries were used very locally and so they were numerous and often very small. Their sites can often still be found through place names such as Quarry Walk or Stonefield. Transporting stone was easier where quarries and building sites were near the sea or a river and the stone for important buildings, such as churches, market halls and mansions, could be shipped.

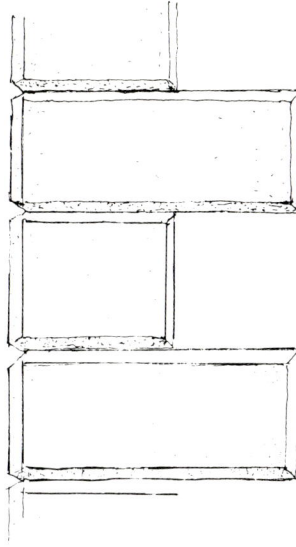

◀ 10 Quoins.

▲
11 Coursed rubble walls.

▲
12 Uncoursed rubble walls.

9

13 Knapped flint.

15 Galleting.

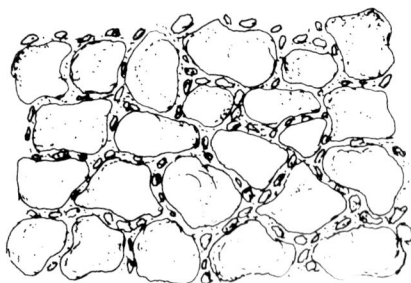

14 Brick quoins.

There was an upsurge of stone building in late Tudor and Stuart times, as yeomen farmers and merchants flourished into a middle class with more money to spend on their homes, and stone was preferred to timber because of fire risk.

Each type of stone has a texture and colour of its own, giving villages and buildings a distinctive look. The Cotswolds are famous for their yellow buildings of *oolitic limestone*. This is a hard limestone formed in the Jurassic period one hundred and forty to one hundred and ninety-five million years ago.

Other examples are Cheshire's pinky fawn millstone grit, Chester's pink keuper sandstone and Norfolk's carstone, a golden brown sandstone. The hard granites are found throughout the highland zone, a pale grey granite in Aberdeen, in Merionethshire a grey blue, red in Leicestershire, pink in Devon and a silver grey in Cornwall. In the Lake District a product of past volcanic activity is *tuff*, derived from compacted volcanic ash, which gives a green local building material. A geology map will indicate the main types of stone in an area, but the colour of the same type of stone can also vary from one quarry to another.

There are also local stones in areas of the lowlands that builders like to use. Kentish ragstone was used to build London's Roman wall, the watergate of the Tower of London and many of London's Victorian churches. Portland stone, a Dorset limestone, was used to rebuild St Paul's Cathedral. These stones were moved from their respective quarries on the River Medway and Portland Bill via the Channel and the Thames to London, using ships to carry the heavy loads.

Flint is a non-porous, hardwearing silica stone found in carboniferous areas and used for building in Norfolk and South East England. Because flints are irregular in shape, they have to be split or *knapped* to give a wall a flat appearance. Bricks are often used with flint, to frame the wall, to make quoins and the final course. Mortar is used to bind the flints together, and chips of flint are

Stone may be cut and shaped by splitting it along natural bedding planes, sawing it or splitting it with wedges, according to its type. *Ashlar* is stone cut precisely into rectangular blocks. This takes time and ashlar is expensive if used exclusively and laid in courses. Therefore, for many smaller homes, ashlar is often only used for the *quoins* — corner stones — and the rest of the walls consist of stone pieces or rubble laid either in courses or uncoursed, as required, and bonded together with mortar.

Working with stone today has not basically changed, although machines now do the heavy lifting, but it is still an expensive material.

10

sometimes pushed into the mortar, a decoration called *galleting*. Galleting is also used on other types of stone wall, using chips of the same material.

Flint houses were popular in the sixteenth century and, after a lapse, revived in popularity in the eighteenth century.

Modern building stone is very expensive because of labour costs, and is often now produced by mixing crushed stone and cement to form blocks to an ordered size and shape. Stone facing is still used, and modern highly polished granite makes an impressive finish to business buildings belonging to banks and insurance companies.

Brick Walls

Brick is now a popular building material throughout Britain, and has become so largely through man's technical evolution in the past two hundred years, not only in making bricks, but in transportation.

Man has made bricks for many thousands of years. The earliest were of unbaked clay in the ancient world. The Spanish word *adobe* has been given to these bricks in modern times, and they were mainly produced in sunny, hot climates. In Britain, timber and stone were the best building materials until the arrival of the Romans at the beginning of the first century. They then introduced their thin tile-like bricks which were baked in clamps, as described later. Normally, these bricks were between two and five centimetres thick, thirty to forty-five centimetres long and fifteen to thirty centimetres wide. Because they were so thin, they baked into a very hard brick, and they survived in good condition long after the Romans left Britain in the fifth century. These Roman bricks were re-used by the Saxons and notably by the Normans, for church building.

English bricks were first made about 1200 AD. They were called the *Great Brick*, measured approximately thirty by forty by five centimetres and were made by *moulding* — using a wooden frame into which the wet clay was shaped — in areas where suitable clay was available. Flemish immigrants in the thirteenth century introduced their own smaller brick, designed to fit a man's hand, twenty-two by ten by five centimetres. Although the bricks, being moulded, should all have been the same size, the moulds were not always filled properly and so hand-made bricks are variable in size. Fourteenth-century Hull was the first town to be built of brick. Its own brick works made bricks a little smaller than the Great Brick.

By the Tudor period brickmaking was growing into an important industry and this was recognized early in the reign of Elizabeth I, when the Tylers and Bricklayers Company was founded in 1557. To try to establish a universal size for bricks, a law was passed in 1571 confirming the size as approximately twenty-two by eleven by five and a half centimetres. However, brick was still expensive for ordinary homes.

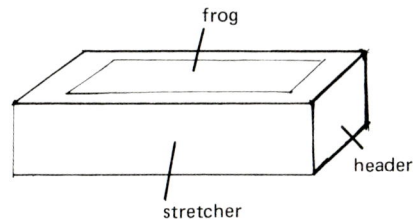

▲
16   Parts of a brick.

▲
17   A brick mould.

▲
18 Eighteenth-century brickmakers.

Until nearly a hundred years ago, before rail transport was established, brickmaking was a seasonal occupation and many brickmakers travelled around the countryside making bricks near to the building sites. This was because of the difficulty in carrying heavy loads on poor roads by horse and cart. Early bricks reflect the colour of the local clays from which they were made.

The brickmaker first dug the brick earth or clay from a site in the ground where it occurred, in the autumn. It was then left to weather through the winter, to enable frost action to break up the lumps. In the spring it was turned and worked with a spade (and bare feet) to give it a "plastic" texture. Moulds were sanded and the clay was packed into them and the top surplus cut away, like dough being put into bread tins. The bricks were emptied carefully from their moulds straightaway, and left to dry for several weeks lying in rows covered with straw. The "green bricks" were laid out in a herringbone fashion, that is at an angle to each other, in piles of up to ten bricks high, called *hacks*.

After this first drying period, they were ready to be fired in *kilns* or *clamps*. Some towns had permanent kilns (ovens), in which bricks were baked hard. Clamp-firing was simpler, however, especially for the travelling brickmaker. A foundation of old fired bricks was laid out, with channels within the foundation for air ducts and spaces for the fuel. Green bricks were laid on the foundation and piled up carefully to leave spaces between them for air and more fuel to be added. Over the now high mound of green bricks an outer layer of mud and old bricks almost sealed the clamp and it was lit from the bottom, heat penetrating throughout the clamp. It could take a week to burn through a clamp of 20,000 bricks. The fuel for the

19 Unstacking a brick clamp.
▼

firings could be turf, but wood faggots were popular till the seventeenth century when coal was used. When the clamp was opened, by breaking up the outer covering of mud, the bricks were sorted into grades. The firing produced varying temperatures in the clamp so that some bricks were harder than others. The hardest bricks were sold for building outer walls and others were sold, according to their grade, for less demanding jobs, but overfired bricks were used to make decorative patterns in brick walls, as they were darker in colour.

The high iron content of some clays, such as those of the Midlands, produced a red brick which was fashionable in the late Tudor period. However, where the clay did not produce red bricks, iron oxide was added in the form of by-products of tanning and brewing. Brick chimneys were also popular in the Tudor period and yeomen farmers added them to timber-framed houses for fashion's sake, as well as for practical use.

▲
20a   Stretcher bond.

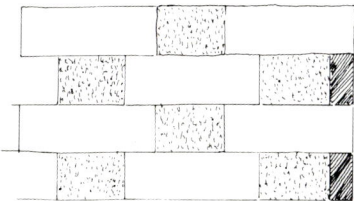

▲
20b   Flemish bond.

20c   English bond.
▼

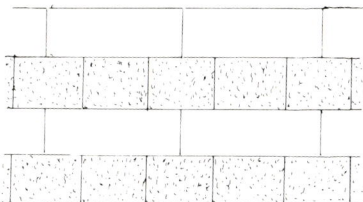

▲
21   A pugmill.

Bricks are mortared together in rows in various ways known as *bonding*.

English bonding — one row *headers*, one row *stretchers* — was a strong popular bond, but in about 1631 Flemish bond was introduced and became fashionable — one brick header, one brick stretcher in each row. The Great Fire of 1666 led to an increase in the use of brick, especially in lowland Britain, and the introduction at the end of the seventeenth century of the pugmill helped to speed brick production. The *pugmill* was in effect a large mixing machine for blending clay and making it ready for moulding. A horse was attached via a beam to a central pivot, that churned the contents of the pugmill as the horse walked round in a circle. In 1707 a bye-law in London made it illegal to have wood showing at the eaves of houses, and so brick parapets were built along and above the eaves.

During Queen Anne's reign, at the beginning of the eighteenth century, red brick with stone quoins was fashionable, but as brick became cheap enough for cottages to be built of it too, red brick declined in fashion and the yellow blends were in vogue! Rubbed bricks were also favoured, to give a carved stone appearance, particularly over windows, and special soft bricks for this purpose were baked. These

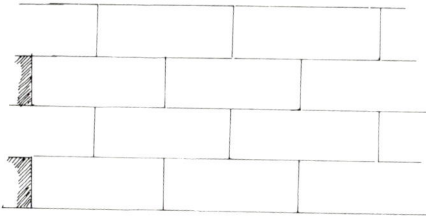

13

soft bricks were sawn to the shape of the design and rubbed with another brick, so that the design seams were hardly seen.

The Brick Tax, 1784-1850

Date		Tax	
1784	1000 green bricks in hacks	2/6	or 12½p
1794	1000 green bricks in hacks	4/-	or 20p
1803	1000 green bricks in hacks small	5/-	or 25p
1803	1000 green bricks in hacks large	10/-	or 50p

22 A Georgian house with string course.
▼

23 A diaper-patterned brick wall.
▼

The Brick Tax was introduced by King George III's new prime minister, William Pitt — Britain's youngest prime minister at twenty-four years of age. The Brick Tax was part of the "ordering and reconstruction of the finances of the nation" (*A History of The English Speaking Peoples* by W. S. Churchill). The effect of the tax, when it was first introduced, was to increase the size of bricks, to nearly that of the Great Brick, as the tax was on quantity not size. However, the third amendment reversed this trend by doubling the tax on large bricks. During the period of the tax, the fashion for stone buildings was strong for wealthier homes, and for smaller houses the use of wall cladding increased; but brick was still a popular building material. In spite of the tax, it was still cheaper than stone and the most practicable for building the town houses and factories now flourishing as people moved from the country to the towns to seek new employment in industry. When the brick tax was lifted in 1850, there was renewed interest in brick and the decorative uses it could offer. *String courses* and quoins in contrasting coloured bricks were fashionable. The Victorians revived the use of grey headers for *diaper* patterns in walls — a fashion from the Tudor period. Grey headers were made by over-firing especially at high temperatures, so that the silica sand in the clay often melted to give a glassy finish to the surface of the brick, which also turned a darker colour than usual.

24 A Hoffmann kiln.
▼

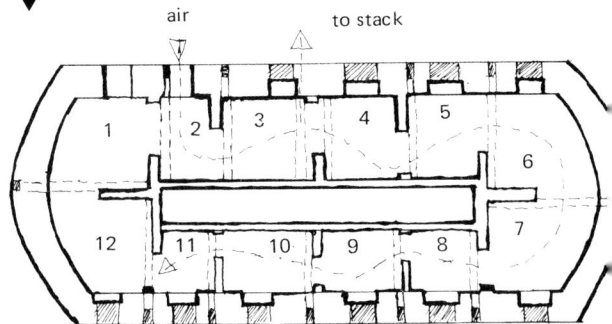

14

The regional coloured bricks could now spread to other areas, as canal and then rail transport "opened up" the land. Before the nineteenth century houses in the Midlands were bright red, in the London area yellow and in the Severn Valley white, while Dorset's houses were purple. For the Victorian house builder, the choice of brick colour was wider.

The new demand for brick for building industrial factories and towns gave an extra incentive to produce even more bricks. Various people invented brickmaking machines which, like the pugmill, were worked by horse-power. The final process in brickmaking was brought up to date in 1858 by the invention of a continuous firing kiln, by an Austrian, Frederick Hoffmann. Until this time clamps and kilns had had to burn out and cool down before being opened to remove the fired bricks, and the process could be started again with green bricks. The *Hoffmann kiln*, however, had a series of chambers, side by side, each one connected to the next by a channel which was packed with paper. Green bricks and fuel were placed in all the chambers. A fire was lit in the first chamber and while the bricks there were baking, the heat and then the fire spread via the connecting channel to the second chamber. The fuel in the second chamber fired and this process continued through all the kiln, until the fire returned to the first chamber, which by this time had been emptied of its fired bricks and repacked with green bricks. Because of the arrangement of the Hoffmann kiln in an oval shape of many chambers, the kiln fires burned continuously for years, used only a quarter of the fuel of previous methods, and gave a better fired result.

In spite of the nineteenth-century inventions that aided the brickmaking process, the people working in the industry had a laborious, tedious life. Men, women and children worked for up to fourteen hours a day in the brickyards. The Factories Act (Brick and Tile Yards) Extension, which came into force in 1872, regulated the employment of women and children, but brickmaking was still an exhausting occupation. One of the unpleasant jobs for North Kent brickmakers was the sorting of London's rubbish. Brick barges returning to Kent from London were filled with refuse, or *"rough stuff"* as it was called, which was dumped in heaps in the brickyard to "mature" for a year. The vegetable and food parts had hopefully rotted by then, leaving ashes from domestic coal fires and broken china and glass to be sifted and sorted by the workers. The fine ash was added to the clay, which can be seen in London's yellow brick, while large ash pieces, *cinders*, which were still burnable, were used to fire the kilns. The remaining material in the rough stuff, such as broken glass and china, was dumped. Rough stuff was used in North Kent brickyards till after the 1939-45 War when central heating by gas and oil, and smokeless fuels, became popular — then rough stuff lost its valued ashes.

The greatest discovery in brickmaking has been the *Fletton brick*. The material used to make this brick is a shale clay called Lower Oxford clay, and lies in a band along the highland and lowland building stone line — Dorset to Yorkshire. In 1881 it was discovered, near the village of Fletton, that Lower Oxford clay could be pressed into shape when partly dry and fired immediately, without the usual few weeks needed for drying out green bricks. The shale clay contained a percentage of oil which helped burn itself, when fired with coal dust, so reducing again the cost of fuel. The Hoffmann kiln proved the best kiln in which to fire flettons, but the short Hoffmann kiln chimney had to be made taller to carry away the extra smoke that "flettons" made.

At the turn of the century a mechanical clay digger was introduced, and mass production of flettons, as we know today, had arrived. One company now makes all the British flettons and half the nation's bricks — The London Brick Company — and the

15

initials *L B C* can be seen stamped on their bricks.

The latest materials for making bricks are sand and lime, moulded under pressure when moist. Sand and cement are another combination of modern materials. The modern bricks are made of a variety of substances and in many colours, with textured surfaces, for different building tasks. Brick is still the most popular building material for ordinary homes.

Wall Cladding and Rendering

Wall cladding and rendering of walls are means whereby walls are covered to protect them from weathering or to change or improve their appearance.

In Tudor times farm buildings and cottages in South Eastern counties were protected by *weather boarding* or *clap board*, to extend the life of a wattle-and-daub-built home. Lengths of thin wooden board, elm or imported soft woods such as pine, were laid horizontally on a wall, so that they overlapped at their lower edge. Often in Tudor times only the upper part of the walls was weather-boarded, but in the Georgian period whole house fronts were covered and this style of cladding was popular for small houses. Red brick houses could change their appearance and become more fashionable to their Georgian owners. Today, weather boarding is still used, but in addition to imported soft wood, cedar wood in its natural reddish colour is popular. Soft wood weather board has always been painted, usually white, but in coastal areas the boards were often tarred on fishermen's cottages, to give better protection from salt air, although modern paints now make tarring unnecessary. Tarred weather boards can still be seen, however, especially on old farm buildings.

Like weather boarding, *weather tiling* or *tile hanging* is most popular in South Eastern counties, and has been since the early Georgian period. The older tile-hung homes are timber-framed houses where the plaster needed extra protection. The tiles are hung on horizontal laths and overlap each other. Brick walls, too, were tile-hung, to protect poor bricks or for decoration. The tiles are made of clay and fired like bricks, and older tiles show local colour variation. Often only a gable or the upper walls are clad, using shaped or rectangular tiles. In Victorian times the *fishscale* shape of tile was a popular cladding and has continued to be so. Tiles are now made of concrete and, besides the original reds, green, yellow, grey and fawn are available in a variety of shapes including hexagons and pentagons — six- and five-sided shapes.

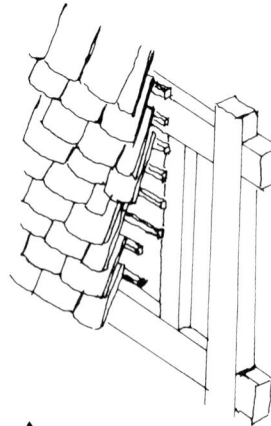

▲
25   Tile hanging.

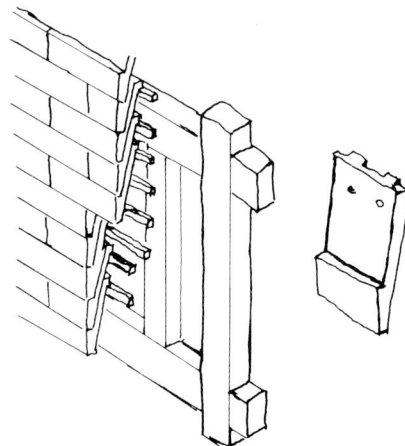

▲
26   Mathematical tiling.

16

Mathematical tiles were mainly produced and used during the period of the Brick Tax (1784-1850). They were hung like the usual tile cladding — nailed to horizontal laths of wood, but they did not overlap and the joints between tiles were mortared to appear like brick bonding — but they were non-taxable. Besides being a wall protection, mathematical tiles were a cheap way to keep up with fashion. Red brick and timber-framed houses were unfashionable in the Georgian period, but yellow or pale-coloured mathematical tiles could be used to hide the offending walls.

Stone facing or *cladding* was also popular in the eighteenth century. Thin "tiles" of smooth limestone or sandstone ashlar were used, but this was still expensive. Today polished granite is a modern cladding for important buildings.

A cheap substitute for stone cladding was *stucco rendering*. The formula for making stucco — which is a hard plaster — was kept a secret, although it was thought to be a blend of sand and fine clay. The plaster was mixed like a smooth cement and spread evenly over the walls; markings were made on the surface to give the appearance of ashlar blocks.

In 1824 the formula for *Portland cement* was patented and this was said to give the walls a Portland stone effect. White *cement rendering* is a modern development. During the past hundred years *pebble dash* finishes have been popular, though now the fashion is declining. Small stones or shingle are thrown onto wet cement-rendered walls to give a rough pebble finish.

Proprietary water-proofing and masonry paints are used to protect many walls today.

The story "behind" walls of houses seen today has progressed from the early practical, physical problems of working with local materials, through to the Georgian period where fashion had a power we may find hard to understand. The modern house builder has a wider choice of materials to use than ever before, but costs are the limiting factor common to all.

2
Roofs

Until roads and transport were greatly improved, a process that did not start until nearly two hundred years ago, roofs, like the rest of the house, were built of local materials. The roof had to be lightweight enough to be supported by the walls and timber frames, but waterproof and durable. In Britain a roof needs to slope, so that rain water and snow can be shed quickly. Flat roofs have not been practical, although, with modern methods and materials, they are now used; but they are not popular for houses. The exact angle of the slope, or pitch, to the roof is influenced by the roofing material.

Thatched Roofs

Thatch originally meant any roof covering, when vegetable material was the only roofing material used. As other roofing materials were introduced, the term "thatch" came to describe only vegetable materials. Thatch roofs were most popular up to the sixteenth century, but the more fire-proof material — clay tiles — increased in favour when they became cheaper and easier to manufacture. However, roofs have continued to be thatched and a few examples can still be seen in Southern Britain.

Straw, reeds, heather, turf or moss are all materials that have been used to cover roofs.

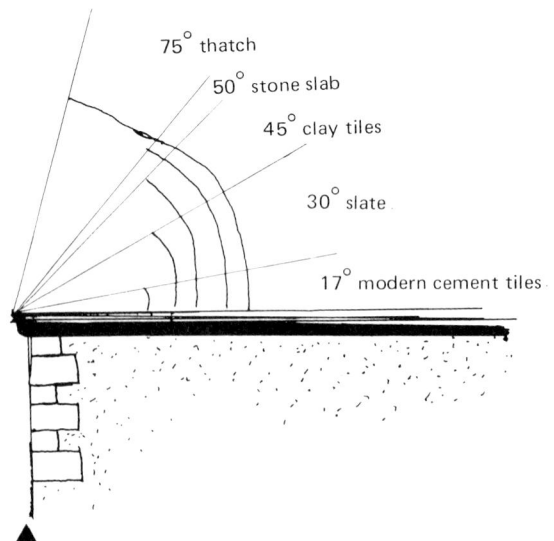

27 Angles of pitch for different roofing materials.

These could be laid on a wooden frame and secured with split twigs — *spars* — and mud. From Celtic times, thatch roofs have been decorated with figures of birds placed at each end of the roof. The figures were made from straw and the tradition still persists in the West Country.

Straw thatch has been a common roofing material, notably in the early nineteenth century when cereal crops with long stems were cultivated and extensively grown. After the seeds had been removed by threshing, the stalks or straw could be used for roofing. Rye straw is considered the strongest and

18

▲
28   A thatch.

can last for thirty years. The art of straw thatching was well-known up to fifty years ago, as it was regularly used by skilled farm workers to thatch haystacks. Modern farming methods in harvesting and gathering in straw have reduced the number of straw thatchers to a few. Machine-cut straw cannot be used for thatching, and to hand-cut it is expensive. The long-stemmed varieties of

29   Figures of birds decorate a thatched roof.
▼

cereal crops are not very often grown, as a shorter-stemmed variety, yielding large seed heads, has been produced. Straw for a modern thatch roof or its replacement has to be especially grown today. An old thatch, when replaced, was dug into the ground as compost, as it had become impregnated with soot and dust over the years and could be recycled as plant food!

Reeds make a longer-lasting roof than straw, up to a hundred years, but a skilled professional thatcher is needed for this work. Reed thatch has been used since before Roman times and is still used to rethatch existing roofs and for a few new houses. The area renowned for reed thatch is Norfolk, but wherever local rivers and marshland grow reeds, this material was, and still is, used. As in the past, reeds are still cut and bundled in winter and those cut from *brackish* (salty) water are considered best, as the salt in the water preserves the reed.

Thatchers around moorland areas, such as Dartmoor, Yorkshire, Northumberland and Scotland, found heather a good material to use. The heather was cut in autumn, while flowering, and laid in layers on laths over roof rafters. Sometimes clay was used to embed the ends of the heather into the next layer. Heather thatch is sometimes used today for roofing summer houses and pavilions.

Turf and moss were also used to roof the poorer homes long before the sixteenth century. It was often used with heather as a base, but only lasted for a year or two.

The *pitch* or slope of a thatch roof has to be steep — up to 75° — so that water can drain quickly and thus prevent the thatch becoming water-logged. Because thatch is light, the large roof area produced by a steep pitch can be supported by normal timbers. There are no gutters to a thatch roof as it is so thick, but this thickness gives good *insulation* to the house, preventing the movement of heat through the roof. A thatched house is, therefore, warm in winter and cool in summer.

19

Where thatch roofs have been replaced by other materials, the steep pitch is noticeable. The gable or end wall will often show brick *tumbling*. To avoid a steep angle being cut into a brick to shape the gable end, whole bricks were placed on their sides sloping downwards. It was wiser to leave handmade bricks uncut, as they were often softer inside and so not hardwearing. When houses were built with stone walls, the cutting of the stone for the gable slope was made unnecessary by placing the stones, like steps, to form the angle, and this is called *crow stepping*.

Although an attractive, useful material, thatch has the major disadvantage of catching fire easily. To help pull down a thatch

30   Brick tumbling.
▼

31   Crow stepping.
▼

that was on fire, long-handled hooks were kept in readiness, and examples can be seen in museums. Some attempt was made to reduce the fire risk by plastering or whitewashing the thatch, but in London thatch roofs were banned in the thirteenth century.

Wooden Roofs

Shingles are wooden tiles, originally made of oblong lengths of oak planks, about thirty centimetres long and fifteen wide. The shingles were thicker at one edge and were shaped to help water to be shed quickly. They were laid so that they overlapped each other well, the thicker edge at the bottom, and were secured to roof battens with oak pegs. Shingle roofs were popular from Roman times, but when timber became less plentiful in the Middle Ages and fireproof materials for roofs were favoured, shingles declined in popularity. Shingle roofs are still occasionally to be seen on houses, and shingles are sometimes used for tall, thin, church spires. Imported cedar is often used for modern shingle tiles. The life expectancy of a shingle roof is up to one hundred years.

Stone Roofs

In the stone-building areas of Britain, where stone can be found that can be split into thin slabs, these were used for covering roofs from Roman times until the nineteenth century. Roman stone slabs were often cut into diamond shapes, but rectangular shapes were more usual after this period.

A stone roof is a very heavy one, and needs strong timbers in the frame of the roof to support it. However, because the slabs are naturally uneven, a pitch of about 50° is necessary, allowing quick drainage, and so avoiding seepage by rain and snow.

Holes were drilled at one end of the slab, a slow job by hand, and the slabs hung on roof battens with wooden pegs or sheep-

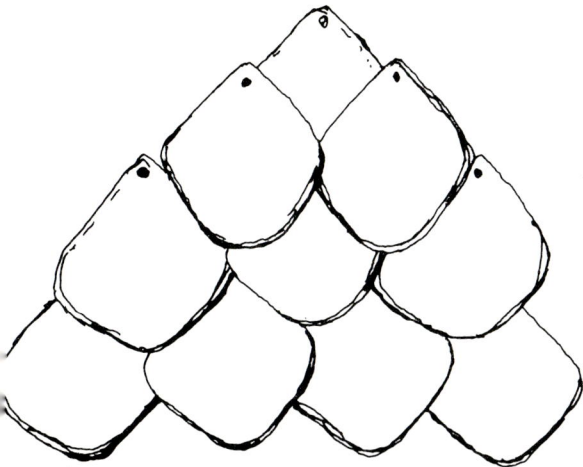

32   Roman stone slabs.

bone pegs. Because of the unevenness of stone slabs, the seams were sealed with moss on top and mortar under the roof. The thickest slabs were used at the eaves and the thinner ones towards the ridge.

Limestone is the most popular stone for roofs and the Cotswolds are famous for their limestone roofs. A means of splitting limestone for roof slabs was discovered in the sixteenth century, which increased the supply of slabs. Large rocks were cut from the quarry in autumn and left to be frosted throughout the winter. The limestone was regularly watered, so that the expansion of ice in the cracks then split the stone and enabled the mason to cut and trim the slabs more easily in the spring. Purbeck limestone was popular in the eighteenth and nineteenth centuries, but was quarried, not frosted, as it split quite readily. The fashion for stone buildings in a non-stone building area was followed in the London area by transporting Purbeck limestone by sea from the Solent to the Thames. The roof timbers need to be particularly strong to support Purbeck stone slabs, and these roofs are often seen today with a distinctive saggy roof line.

Sandstone makes another good roofing slab and was used throughout the stone building areas. In the Northern counties regional variations in the sandstone gave

distinction to local slabs or flagstones — Elland flagstones of the Huddersfield, Bradford and Halifax areas, Rossendale flags and "Thackstones" from the Colne Valley. Millstone grit is another popular roofing slab seen in Cheshire villages.

Although stone slabs are no longer widely used for roofing, there are many houses of long standing which still carry their regional stone roof. Stone slabs are required to repair these roofs and for roof extensions and for a few new houses wishing to blend into a stone built village. The recycling of stone roof slabs is a very popular way of obtaining stone slabs, as quarrying has declined.

Slate Roofs

A most commonly recognized roofing material is *Welsh slate*. Welsh slate was popular from the end of the eighteenth century, as it was very light, needing only a lightweight and, therefore, cheaper wooden frame to support it. It was widely used as a roofing material for the buildings rapidly erected during the Industrial Revolution. The slates were quarried and, in skilled hands, split readily into thin roof tiles. Two sizes of slate were popular: the "duchess", which measured sixty by thirty centimetres, and the "countess", measuring forty-five by thirty centimetres. Two holes were drilled at one end and one on either side, halfway down. The slates were placed, overlapping each other, on the roof battens and nailed into place with iron nails. Iron nails, however, rust after a hundred years and Victorian slate roofs now need to be replaced with tiles or the slates rehung with rustproof nails. Because of their light weight, slate roofs have a shallow pitch of $30° - 45°$.

The popular Victorian Welsh slate was not the only type of slate used for roofing. Slate from Devon was used in the Middle Ages and was shipped to many areas of South East England. Cornish and Leicestershire slates were popular in the eighteenth century.

These slates were thicker and varied in colour from the Welsh slate, but were good roofing materials. In the Lake District, local slate is still used and gives a greenish colour to the roofs.

Tile Roofs

Tile making began in the thirteenth century in the South East of England where there was need for a fireproof roofing material. The *clay tile* was shaped in the style of the wooden shingle — an oblong with a curved surface — then fired in clamps or kilns like a brick. Many of the early clay tiles were imported from Flanders, but the British tile making industry was well established when in 1477 laws were made to regulate the size of a tile to approximately twenty-six by fifteen by one centimetres. Sizes still varied for the hand-made tile, as they did for bricks, and a further law was needed in 1725 to confirm the size of plain tiles — simple oblong clay tiles — as opposed to pantiles, slate or stone slabs. Clay tiles were hung on horizontal battens with wooden pegs, and old tiles have two square holes at one end where the square pegs fitted, which are a useful guide to the origin of the tile. They also show colour variation due to local clays and uneven firing. Towards the end of the nineteenth century the tile design was altered to include *nibs*, two clay projections formed near the nail holes, which were now rounded to fit manufactured round nails. The "nibbed" tile could be hung over the roof battens. Tiles are double-lapped when laid, so that there are two thicknesses of tile over the roof — which makes a plain tile roof heavier than one might have suspected. Not all the courses are nailed to battens where there are nibs. Every third course is nailed in roofs that are exposed to winds; otherwise, every fifth course is nailed. The pitch of a clay roof is 45°. Improving manufacturing techniques made tiles much cheaper from the seventeenth century, when tile roofs rapidly replaced thatch and shingle.

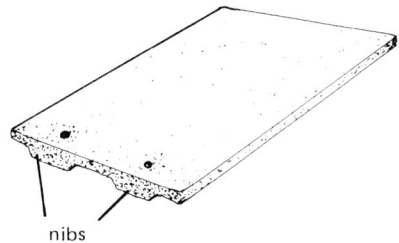

nibs

▲
33   A nibbed tile.

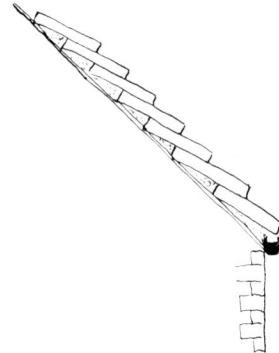

34   Double-lapped plain tiles, seen from the gable end.

Pantiles are an "S"-shaped clay tile, imported in the seventeenth century from Holland, but manufactured in England from 1701. Pantile roofs were popular in areas trading with Holland, such as East Anglia and Bridgwater in Somerset, and were fashionable in the Georgian period when low-pitched roofs were desired. The pantile was larger than a plain tile — thirty-four by twenty-four by one and a half centimetres. Although they looked a heavy roofing material, the tiles were only laid in single lap, as they fitted into each other at the curved part of the "S" with grooves, so making a waterproof seam. The roof was, therefore, lighter than a plain tile one and the pitch could be lower, at 30°.

The twentieth-century manufactured *cement tile* is made in various shapes, colours and sizes and gives an even, uniform surface to a roof. Some tiles are made larger than the standard size, to be used on roofs with as low a pitch as 17°. Tiles are still secured with nails to battens on timber rafters, and red is still a popular colour, a reminder of hand-made clay tiles of the Tudor and Jacobean periods. Green, beige and grey colours are also seen now and, although the plain rectangular tile is dominant, pantiles and squared ridged variations of the pantile are available.

Lead

Lead has been used on flat roofs and in small sheets on expensive or important buildings since Roman times. But lead is, and always has been, an expensive metal, although its softness and pliability make it useful for sealing joins between chimneys and roofs, window frames and walls and for guttering. A roof covered in lead is very rare.

Composition Tiles

Square or diamond-shaped tiles were made from a thin tar-like substance called bitumen, often of a pinkish colour, in the early twentieth century. Houses built about the period of the First World War, with this kind of roof, are easily recognized by the diamond patterning and the flat, even surface.

Corrugated Roofs

Corrugated metal and asbestos roofs are of twentieth-century origin. These materials are usually used on farm buildings, often replacing a thatched roof, and for garage roofs. Some houses built between the wars may also have a corrugated roof.

Roof Ridges

Where the ridge pole spans the roof, between gable ends, lies the *roof ridge*. This has to form a water-tight joint between the two

▲
35   Crested ridge tiles.

parts of the sloping roof. On thatched roofs a capping of a different material to that of the roof is often used, such as a sedge ridge on a reed thatch. *Sedge* is a short, tough member of the group of plants to which grass and reeds belong, and it grows in damp areas.

Stone-slab roofs are ridged with specially cut stone blocks from which a wedge has been removed, leaving an "L"-shaped length to cap the ridge. Slate roofs use stone ridge cappings or moulded clay ridge tiles.

Clay tile roofs and those of slate were often decorated in the Victorian period with crested ridge tiles. Some modern, all-electric homes have a few ridge tiles designed to act as roof ventilators.

Roof Shapes

The two main types of roof shape are the *gabled* and the *hipped*. Gable roofs were the main shape, originated by cruck-timber frames — the "A" shape. The angle of the slope of the roof dictated the width of rooms below. A gable can be extended lengthwise to make terrace houses.

The hipped roof shape was used from the seventeenth century to make more room in the roof, and was fashionable in the Georgian period as it could be used to make shallow pitched roofs. Hipped roofs used shorter ridge poles, which was also an advantage as long timbers were scarce.

Combinations of the hipped and gabled

23

36 A hipped roof.

37 Gabled and hipped styles combined.

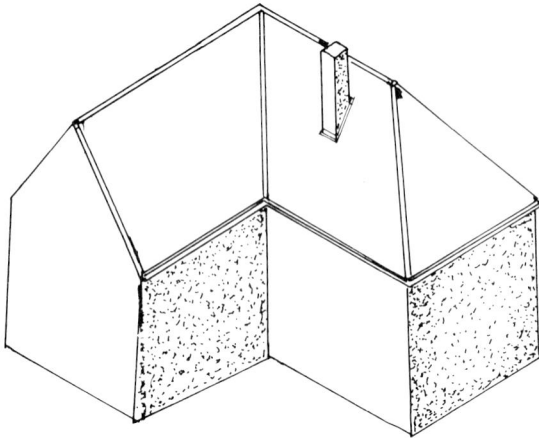

38 Valleys joining roofs.

39 A Mansard roof.

a French architect in the late seventeenth century and gave increased height to attic rooms. The lower half of the roof had a much steeper pitch than the upper half. Slate and clay tiles were the roofing materials used to cover this shape. Lincolnshire and Norfolk have more examples of older houses with this roof shape than elsewhere, but a more exaggerated form of Mansard roof can be seen in modern houses. Hence today's large dormer windows and almost vertical lower roof do not reflect the original Mansard roof's likeness to the hull of a Spanish galleon.

Decorated Gable Ends

In the Middle Ages the end gables were often decorated with beautifully carved boards outlining the "A" shape. These were called *bargeboards*. In the nineteenth century the Victorians revived the fashion, but the

styles were used for larger houses, and the different roofs were joined along the eaves with a gutter, or by a small area of flat roof covered with lead, or with special ridge tiles called "saddle backs". Sloping gutters or *valleys*, to join roofs set at right angles to each other, were lined with half-rounded tiles or lead.

A less frequently used shape of roof is the *Mansard roof*. This was a shape designed by

40 Decorated bargeboards.

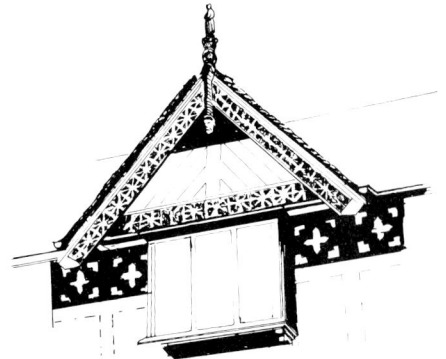

41 Dutch gables.

ceal the roof, by heightening the front wall to form a *parapet*, or to make a *balustrade* of small pillars behind which a low-pitched roof could be hidden. Behind the parapet, gutters could carry rain water to downpipes. Eaves were also decorated with a row of tooth-like projections of white painted blocks of wood or projecting alternate header ends of bricks, called dentilations. *Dentils* were particularly fashionable in the Georgian period.

carvings were not so elaborate. Plain barge-boards still apear on the gable ends of modern houses.

In the seventeenth century decorative curves in brick and stone formed the basic triangular shape of the gable and this was a copy of a Dutch style. The *Dutch gable* was also used on the front of buildings, and East Anglian houses were influenced by this fashion, because of their trading links with Holland.

Eaves

Where the roof joins the vertical walls of a house are the *eaves*. From the late seventeenth century it was fashionable to emphasize the front of the house and to con-

Gutters

Thatch roofs do not need gutters, as the rain water can drip slowly and evenly off the roof, and a thatch is rather too thick for gutters to be economically made for it. A tiled roof channels the rain water, which runs quickly down its slope, and from the thirteenth century, especially in towns, roof pipes were used to discharge rain water directly from the roof into the streets below. In the Tudor period gutters and downpipes were used to collect and store rain water in tanks. Piped water to houses was unknown at this time and drinking water had to be bought from water-sellers in the towns or drawn from communal wells and pumps. A supply of rain water was, therefore, most useful. The first pipes and gutters were made

42 A parapet with dentils partly concealing a Georgian hipped roof.

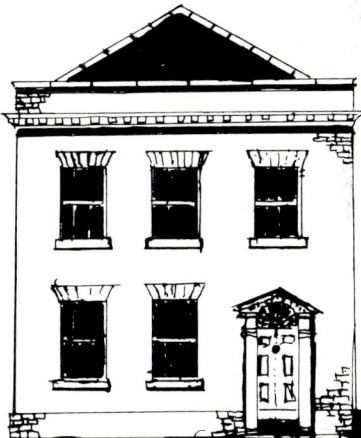

43 Decorated rain-water heads.

of wood lined with tar. Richer homes of the late sixteenth century had square downpipes made of lead, with the rain-water heads, the collecting sections at the top of the downpipes, often elaborately decorated. In the Georgian period this decoration declined, as the gutters were concealed to enhance the symmetry of the front of the houses.

As the Industrial Revolution expanded the production of manufactured items, cheap cast-iron downpipes were available from the end of the eighteenth century. The twentieth century has seen the introduction of asbestos guttering and downpipes and the latest material, PVC, plastic.

Fire-break Walls

Often, in a terrace of houses, several low walls will be seen projecting above the roof, demarcating the separate homes. These are fire-break walls, which were made compulsory from the seventeenth century. The party walls have to be extended through and above the roof, to prevent fire spreading along a terrace of houses via the roof space. Good examples of fire-break walls can be seen in some Victorian terrace houses.

44   A fire-break wall.
▼

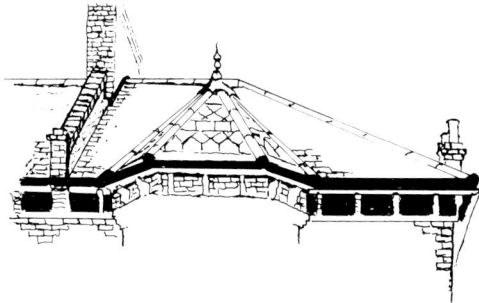

Dormer Windows

Dormer windows are part of a roof and break the uniform roof line. They are windows set in the roof so that light can enter rooms in the roof space, the attics. The window can be set above or below the eaves or halfway across them. Dormer windows also require a small roof, similar to that of the house roof, and this can be a gabled, hipped, flat or raking roof. A raking roof joins the dormer window to the main roof ridge. In thatched roofs the "eyebrow" dormer is an attractive feature. Dormer windows became popular from the seventeenth century and are still popular, although modern dormers are often large and take the place of first-floor windows.

To have "a roof over one's head" is a saying which suggests the reassurance there is in having somewhere to live and belong to. It shows that man has a regard for his home. Traditionally, the roof of a house belonged to the tenant and the walls belonged to the landlord. If the tenant moved house, he could take the roof with him. This could never have been easy, and it is two hundred years since the right was last exercised!

45   Dormer windows placed at the eaves, with gabled, tiled roofs.
▼

3
Doors

In Saxon homes, when domestic animals and man lived under one roof, both people and animals used the one doorway to enter the building. The simplest way to close the opening was by hanging a length of animal skin, a hide, or a piece of coarse material across the gap. This early door could be rolled up and secured with a piece of twine, when the doorway was to be left open. Doorways were the only source of light in the dwelling during the day and the saying "do not darken my doorway again", meaning "don't come to my house again", originates from this period.

The first solid doors were made of a series of vertical planks of wood, held together by cross pieces. The door was hung — that is, fixed vertically to one side of the doorway — by metal straps on metal pins secured to the wall. Another way to "hang" doors was to insert wooden or metal spikes, one at the top and one at the bottom of the door, to one side, and place them in holes at the top and bottom of the doorway, so that the door could pivot, to open and close. Draughts were able to get into the house all round the ill-fitting door, as there was no proper door frame as we know it. There were few rooms and often no internal doors in the simple medieval home.

By the early sixteenth century door frames were fitted around doorways, so reducing draughts. A typical door in a timber-framed

46   A pivot-hung solid door.

47   A sixteenth-century arched door.

◀ 48   Ashlar jambs.

house was set in an arched frame made by two pieces of wood which had been selected from trees that naturally curved. The vertical posts of wood forming the sides of the door frame, the jambs, were often carved. In the

27

late Tudor period, the carving of the door frame could become very elaborate, especially in richer homes. The home was now made up of several rooms, and internal doors similar to the main door were incorporated.

Door frames in stone-built homes had *ashlar blocks*, cut stone cubes, forming the jambs and either a flat stone *lintel* over the door or an arch with a *keystone* as the central support stone. The stone door frame could also be carved if the owner could afford this work. However, some poorer stone houses would have had a simple timber door frame, rather than an expensive ashlar or carved stone one.

Because the doorways now had frames, *flat hinges* could be used to secure the door to the frame. These were made by black-smiths, as the hinges needed to be strong to support the solid wood door. Flat hinges were often ornate, and examples of ornate flat hinges can still be found on church doors. Keys and locks, as we know them, have been used since Roman times, but were expensive as they had to be especially made by the blacksmith. Only a rich home would have a lock, but the poor home was well secured by a wooden *draw bar* across the door. Internal doors could be secured by a *sneck latch*, which opened by pulling on a string to lift a wooden latch on the opposite side of the door.

The Tudor-style framed doorway was still in use well into the seventeenth century, although the simpler square-headed door frame, rather than the arched, became more fashionable. The door frames of flint- or pebble-walled houses were now made of

50   A wooden draw bar fastening.

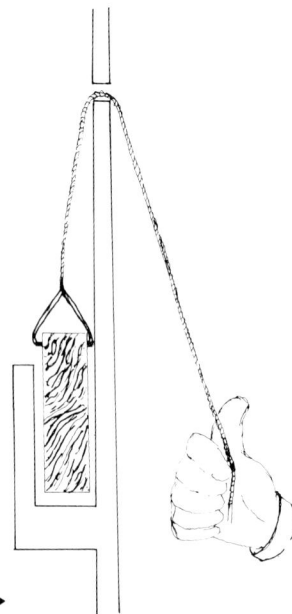

51   A sneck latch. ▶

49a   A simple flat hinge.
▼

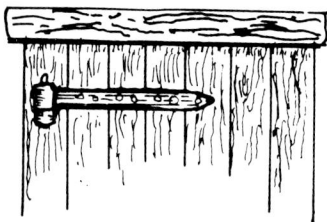

49b   An ornate flat hinge.
▼

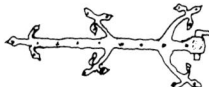

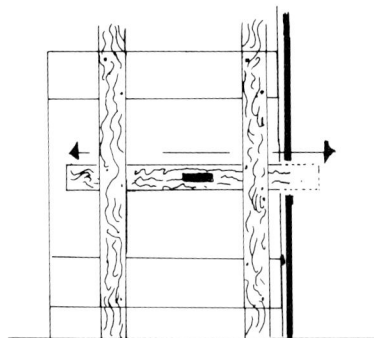

▲
52   Brick jambs for the door of a flint house.

28

▲
53 A panelled door.

▲
54 A canopied door.

▲
55 A spider's web fanlight.

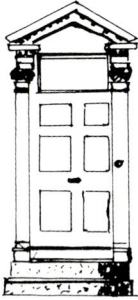

▲
56 An eighteenth-century door with a pediment
and pilasters.

▲
57 A "broken" pediment door frame decoration.

brick, as brick was becoming cheaper and timber more scarce. Timber, especially pine wood, had been imported since medieval times, but now the imports were increasing. Carpenters had to find ways of making the best use of their timber, especially the shorter lengths, and as their skills improved, the solid wooden door declined in favour. Doors were made by fitting four or six panels of wood together into a framework of short timbers. This made a lighter door which could be hung from the door frame by *"H" hinges.*

By the end of the seventeenth century the fashion for symmetrical building styles made front doors a central feature of the home. A typical front door of the Queen Anne period had a *canopy* over it and was flanked by pillars to emphasize the entrance. Poorer homes did not follow fashion, but reflected the trends: in time, as solid doors became too expensive, panelled doors were used.

The front door was still a feature to be highlighted in the eighteenth century. Glass windows over the front door were introduced, to give more light in the hallway within the house. The semi-circular *fanlight* was fitted with *leaded lights*, in various patterns. A popular style was the spider's web, and this was typical of the Georgian house. In the late eighteenth century some of the small upper wooden panels of the door were replaced with glass. The position of the front door was stressed by curved arches, triangular canopies (pediments) and columns (pilasters). *Iron butt hinges* were introduced, and were fixed inside the frame of the door, thus concealing the hinge. These are the same type of

29

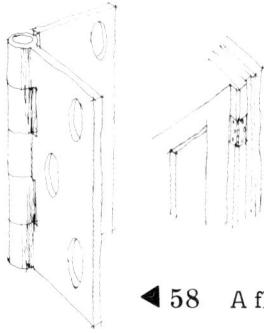

58 A flat butt concealed hinge.

59 A Victorian recessed porch and panelled door.

60 A keyhole porch.

hinges used on most doors today.

At the beginning of the nineteenth century – the Regency period — wooden trellised porches and balconies, decorated by fine wrought-iron *trellis-work*, were fashionable. An upper room or landing, with a window overlooking the main door, might have a wrought-iron balcony, supported by the pillars that emphasized the doorway. This was thought to give an elegant appearance to the house and was a fashionable feature of Regency houses of richer people. By the mid-nineteenth century terraced and semi-detached Victorian villas were being built in great numbers. Doors were mass-produced and were usually four-panelled. The upper two panels of doors for villa-style homes were frequently replaced with coloured or obscure glass. This style of house often had a porch recessed into the hallway, with a patterned obscure glass or coloured glass fanlight over the door. Lintels over doorways, and windows, were in decorative brick. Many industrial-style terrace houses, however, had simple wood panelled front doors, leading straight into the living room from the street.

During the first half of the twentieth century council house estates and private housing estates flourished. Mass-produced panelled doors with approximately one third of the area fitted with small panes of obscure glass, were popular. Recessed porches were still in fashion in both council and private houses. The *keyhole porch* was a distinctive style in some areas of the country, and locks were a standard door fitting.

The second half of the twentieth century has seen a more experimental approach to popular house building and the appearance of an all-glass panelled door set in an aluminium frame — the glass is still obscure, but in varied patterns. Some of these doors slide open, the *patio style*, but the traditional vertical hinged *casement* opening is still dominant.

The modern front door is still mainly wooden framed and panelled, although glass

30

may form a major part of the door material. But the choice of styles is wide. Door locks have become more complex to resist illegal entry.

Interior doors, which had been made in panelled wood since the eighteenth century, are now more likely to be made of a light timber framework covered with hardboard.

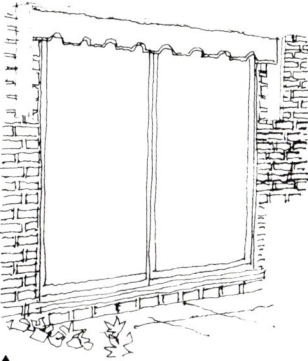

▲
61 A patio style sliding door.

Door Furnishings

Painted cast-iron door knockers and pull handles were introduced in the eighteenth century. On the outside walls, by the door, of some houses of this period brackets may be found for torches and snuffers. Torches, made of short lengths of wood with material soaked in tallow (fat) fastened to one end, were lit and used to light the way after dark. Street lighting was very limited at this time. Snuffers were large metal cones which were put over the torches to extinguish them on arrival at the house. Small snuffers were used inside the house to put out candles, and examples may be seen in museums and private collections.

In the mid-nineteenth century door numbers, names and letterboxes were added to doors, to aid the delivery of letters under the, then new, penny post system. Old doors of the pre-postal age had to have slots cut into the door when letterboxes were required and this shows if the symmetry of the door

▲
62 A bell-pull.

is unbalanced by the letterbox. Cast-iron boot scrapers and mechanical bell-pull knobs were also popular in the Victorian period. Modern doors often have electric lamps outside, electric bell-push buttons and security locks, so that there is a great variety of door furnishings seen today.

Because doors have been made of wood until very recent times and are a well-used feature of a house, their life span is often much shorter than that of the walls. Replacement doors are, therefore, very common and are frequently in a different style to the original door. Very old doors, i.e. over two hundred years, are few and, therefore, doors are a feature to be dated with care. Regional differences and individual differences of old doors are worth recording before the doors are changed. Modern doors have a uniformity that is easy to recognize in all parts of the country, but the door furnishings are more variable as house owners strive for some individuality. Modern doors are painted in a wide range of colours, evidence of the great improvement in paint colours that will resist weathering. Fifty years ago, black, brown, green, cream and white were favoured for outdoor paint colours, but modern doors can be in a rainbow choice of colours as well as in numerous styles and made of many different materials!

63 A boot scraper.
▼

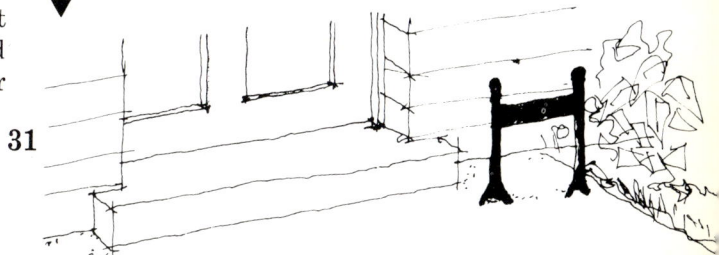

4
Windows

The name window is thought to have come from "wind-hole" or "wind-eye", a hole in the wall, in the prevailing wind side of the house. In Saxon times, these holes were needed to give a good draught of air to the central fireplace. A *window ledge* sloped outwards, to shed rain, and the hole was partially blocked with crisscrossed reeds, a wickerwork of woven twigs or vertical slats about eight to fifteen centimetres apart. This was necessary to keep out birds and other animals. In later medieval times, sliding or hinged wooden *shutters* were introduced, to close the wind-hole, and it began to be used to let in light as well as air. In many homes the open central fireplace was replaced by more efficient hearths set by the wall, with chimneys to take away the smoke. The role of the window changed.

In timber-framed houses a gap (a *pan*) was left between two vertical posts in the wall, to be partly filled by wattle and daub and the remainder formed the wind-hole. So arose the name *"window pane"*. This position for the window can still be seen in some Tudor box-framed houses. The size of the window pane was kept as small as possible because of cold draughts. Up to the end of the sixteenth century, in ordinary homes, oiled fabric or parchment, thin horn or animal placentas were used to fill in the window, but still let in some light. The part of the animal placenta used was the thin,

translucent skin that surrounds an unborn mammal and which is shed after the birth.

Glass had been used in Roman times and the Romans could make rolled glass sheets, but the knowledge was lost when they departed in the fifth century. Not until the nineteenth century did rolled glass appear to be made again in Britain, and it will be described later. The Normans imported European glass for use in churches and important houses. Church windows were typically long with a pointed arch at the head during the thirteenth century, which is now known as the Early English period. This style is called a *lancet window*. By the turn of the fourteenth century, lancet windows were grouped together in twos and threes and more decoration was added to the frames of the upper part of the window. *Drip stones* were built over the windows to prevent rain running over them from the walls above. Later in the fourteenth century stones surrounding the outside of church windows were very ornately carved to give a tracery effect, a lace-like appearance. Stone houses of richer people reflected this style — the Gothic style — which was to be revived for a period in the nineteenth century.

The pieces of glass which were used in these windows were small, about hand size, and were joined together with lead strips to make a window pane, or *"light"*. These were set in a framework of iron. Windows that

▲
64   A slatted window with wooden mullions and shutters.

▲
66   A leaded light casement window.

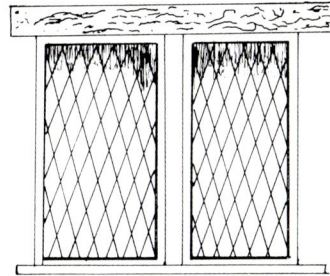

▲
65   A lancet window.

opened were hung from vertically positioned hinges, opening like doors, and were called *casement windows*.

Because the window was expensive, it was placed high up in the wall, so that it could not easily be stolen. People who could afford to have glass windows removed them from their frames when they moved house, and took them with them, together with their furniture. As windows became larger and a feature of the house, their removal became impracticable and so in 1579 laws were passed prohibiting this practice. Windows became a permanent feature of the house.

The windows in large brick Tudor houses had diamond or square-shaped *leaded lights* — panes of glass — which formed a grid pattern. They were set in carved stone vertical *mullions* and horizontal *transoms* — the window surrounds. Over the windows, decorated drip stones were set in the wall. Timber-framed houses had carved wooden window surrounds, while stone houses hung their iron-framed windows on stone mullions. Bay windows became popular and when these were put in rooms on upper floors, they were called *"oriel" windows*. Poorer homes retained wood-framed windows covered with oiled parchment, but yeomen farmers and merchants could afford some glass and a simpler style of the richly decorated Tudor window. Superstitious

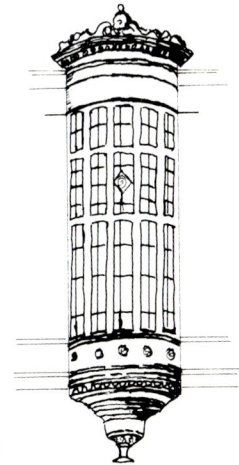

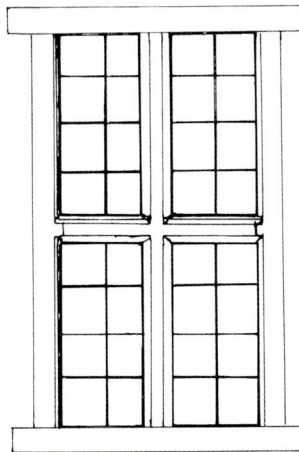

▲   ▲
67   Transoms and mullions. 68   An oriel window.

Elizabethans thought that the plague disease was carried by southerly winds, so they did not build windows in the southern walls of their homes.

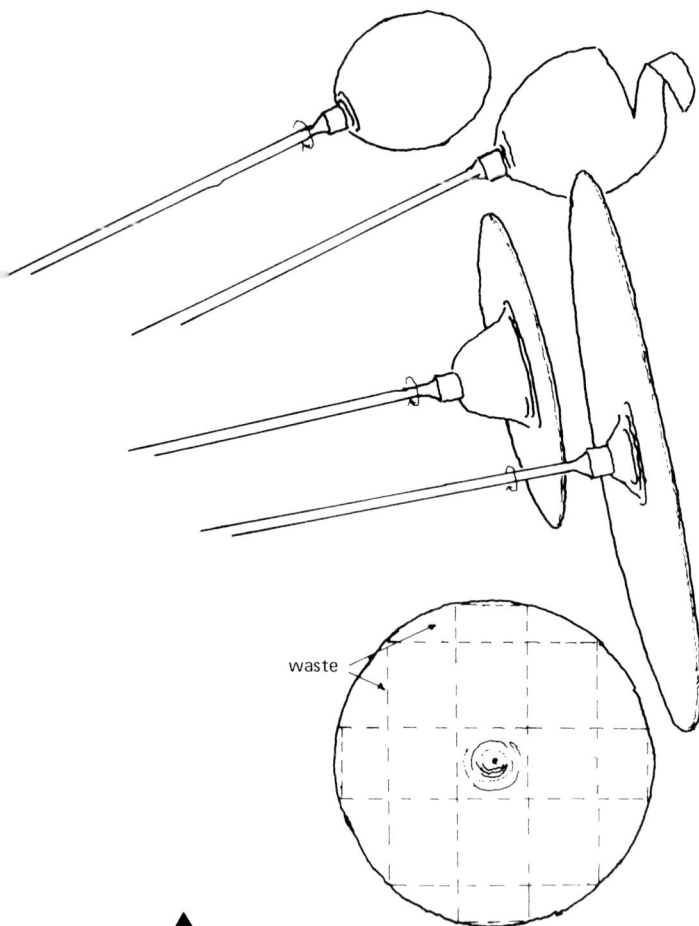

69 The making of crown glass.

waste

made in this manner was known as *crown glass*. The centre square cut from the disc was thick, with a circular mark of the punty on it, and was called the *bullion*. This was discarded or sold cheaply. But today bullion panes are becoming popular in mock-Georgian window frames.

Another popular way to make glass panes was from cylinders of glass or "*muffs*". These were made by first blowing a glass balloon, then cutting away the balloon's base. By alternately blowing and cooling the balloon, an elongated tube or cylinder was formed, which was cut down one side, opened out, flattened and cut into shape as it cooled.

In 1615 James I forbade wood to be used in glass manufacture, as the woodlands and forests were rapidly being used up. The glass makers had to use coal to fire their furnaces, and so they moved to coal mining areas of Britain, to ease transport costs. Fortunately, coal furnaces produce greater heat than wood-burning furnaces and gave a better quality of glass.

In the late seventeenth century, about 1680, *sash windows* were introduced from Holland. The thin iron window frames could not take the strain and weight of sash windows, so wooden window frames were made. Early sash windows had the top half fixed, so that only the lower half could be raised and lowered, and this was secured by a hook. In 1709 a law was passed requiring all wooden frames to windows to be set back in the wall, as a precaution against fire — drip stones were then no longer necessary.

Dormer windows were inserted into roofs, to give light to attics, from the late seventeenth century. These rooms were often the servants' bedrooms. Dormer windows could be set in the roof above the eaves, or below the eaves or midway between roof and wall, on the eave. The dormer window had its own roof, which, like the main house roof, could be hipped, gabled or flat. If the dormer roof extended from the roof ridge to the window, it was called a *raking roof*. The

Glass has been produced in Britain since the thirteenth century, but it was not until the sixteenth century that its manufacture became widespread. Large quantities of wood were used for fires to melt the very pure clean sand, soda ash and limestone into a molten mass. A knob of molten glass was gathered onto the end of an iron tube, and the glass maker blew down the tube into the molten glass which swelled up like a balloon. The balloon of glass was then transferred to another iron rod, a *punty*, which was spun round so that a disc was formed from the balloon of glass. When cool, the disc or "crown", as it was called, was cut into pieces and set into lead frames — "cames". Glass

sides of the dormer window — the *cheeks* — were often tile-hung or weather-boarded.

The seventeenth century saw the expansion of cottage industries, such as spinning and weaving. Upper rooms of the home were made into work rooms and the extra light needed for weaving, for example, was provided by continuous long rows of windows in the upper walls of the house. These were quite distinctive and some good examples can still be seen in Yorkshire of *"weaver's windows"*.

During the eighteenth century "counterbalanced" *sash windows* were introduced, so that both top and bottom halves of the windows could be opened without being secured by hooks. This led to tall elegant windows, which suited the classic symmetrical house designs of the period, as seen in fashionable large houses of the Queen Anne and Georgian styles. In smaller homes, with smaller windows, the horizontal sliding windows were popular. They were designed by a Yorkshireman, early in the eighteenth century — hence the name *Yorkshire sliding sash*. Casement windows were still preferred for homes built of stone, and cast-iron casement window frames continued to be made for cottages, into the nineteenth century.

The Georgian period is also known for its *arched, bowed and barrel window* shapes — the latter being popular for shop fronts.

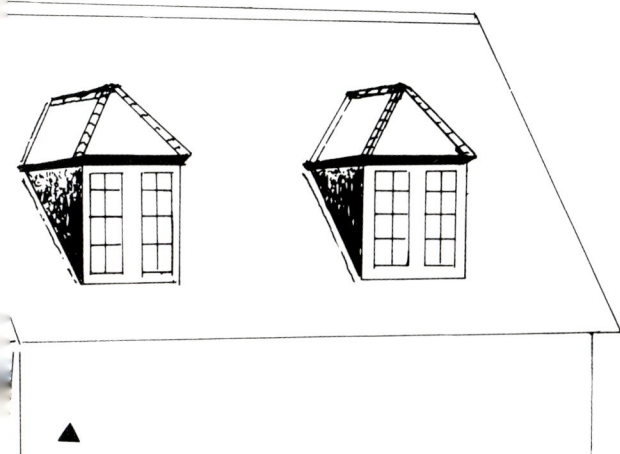

▲

70 Dormer windows.

71 A weaver's cottage.

▼

72 A sash window.

▼

The Window Tax, introduced in 1697, continued to be levied up to 1851 and was charged on houses with more than six windows. This tax did not apply to poorer homes, as they seldom had so many!

Window Tax charged annually 1697-1851

Number of Windows	Tax
0-6	No Tax
7-9	10 new pence
10-19	30 new pence
Over 20	50 new pence

Not all windows that have obviously been bricked up were blocked to avoid paying tax. In restoration or alteration of houses, window and door positions are sometimes changed and the old positions bricked up.

The fashion for symmetry in the eighteenth century led the owners of some large houses to have windows made and placed on brick walls, to give the appearance of real windows. These were called "dummy windows" and were used to balance features of the house.

The abolition of the window tax in 1851 happily coincided with the opening of the Great Exhibition of that year, held in the Crystal Palace, a building largely constructed of sheet glass.

Sheet glass was first produced in 1838 and allowed even the poorest Victorian home to have large, cheaply made, glass windows. Glass conservatories became popular and stained glass pieces were inserted into windows and doors. *Sheet glass* was made by passing molten glass between a series of rollers in a continuous flow. The glass was cut off into lengths, when cooled, at the end of the process. *Victorian sash windows* were simpler and lighter, with fewer transoms and mullions. Drip stones were revived in the Victorian Gothic period and angled bay windows were typical of the suburban villa.

Early twentieth-century windows could be either sash windows or wooden-framed casement windows, which were mass-produced for housing estates. Bathrooms were now being purpose-built into homes

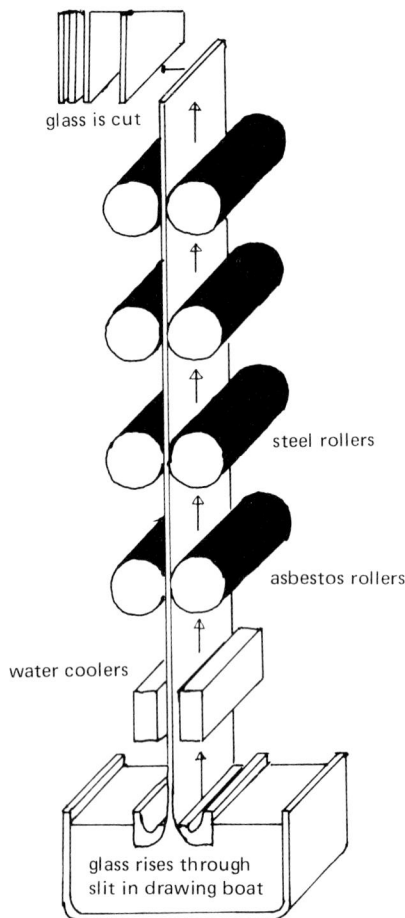

73   The making of sheet glass.

and special obscure glass windows were made for them. Metal frames appeared again in the mid-twentieth century and the aluminium frame is now very common.

The manufacture of large sheets of glass, over a metre square, for *picture windows*, has become possible only since 1959, at an economical rate for ordinary homes. Before the new "float" process was devised, large windows, for shop fronts for example, were made from *plate glass*. This was sheet glass that had been ground and polished and made even. Ordinary sheet glass was too uneven for large windows. *"Float glass"* is flatter

74 An early twentieth-century window.

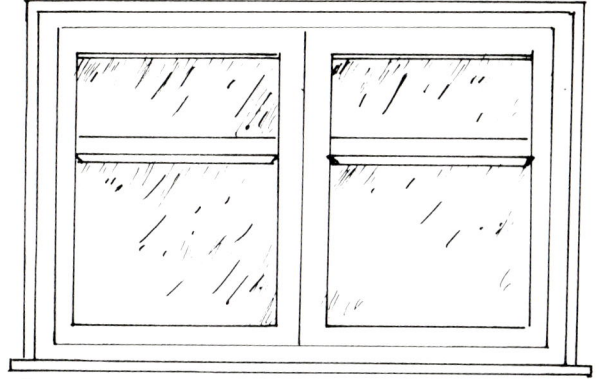

75 A late twentieth-century window.

than plate glass and is made by floating molten glass on a huge bath of liquid tin. One side is smooth from lying against the tin, the other is flattened by heat above it. This makes a better window than plate glass, much more cheaply.

Modern windows copy all the styles that have gone before. In addition, there are the new *pivoted frames* and *picture windows*. Secondary glazing and vacuum-sealed double-glazed windows are evidence of the current concern for fuel conservation. Windows which let through a draught — wind-holes — are, as through the ages, to be avoided!

5
Chimneys

Roman houses in Britain had chimneys that we could recognize today and underfloor heating, but, after the departure of the Romans in the fifth century, the central open hearth of the British was the only type of fireplace.

In Anglo-Saxon cruck houses, open fireplaces were laid on the beaten earth floor in the centre of the main living room. If suitable stone was available, a stone slab formed the hearth, on which wood, charcoal or turf could be burnt, to provide heat for cooking and warmth. The smoke escaped through a hole in the centre of the roof, or through vents left in the gable ends.

To prevent rain and snow entering through the *smoke hole*, the richer homes and Saxon halls had the hole in the roof covered by a *"louvre"*. This was a box-like structure with sides made of a series of horizontal strips — the louvres. They could be opened or closed by pulling a long string, which hung down into the room below. The top of the box was thatched like the roof.

The louvre was not fireproof and, in the thirteenth century, laws attempted to reduce the fire risk by requiring louvres to be plastered over, the thatch as well as the woodwork. By the fourteenth century experiments were made in louvre design to improve smoke extraction: the louvre box was mounted so that it could be moved, like the modern chimney cowls, to take advantage of the wind. Pottery louvres were also made and poorer homes could use a wooden barrel, placed over the roof hole, to help carry away the smoke.

Some purpose-built *chimney-pots* were being made in medieval times. They were a low, conical shape, with triangular vents

76   A smoke hole in the roof of a Saxon house.
▼

77   A smoke hole covered by a louvre.
▼

around the sides, glazed in dark green.

Chimney was a word used in the thirteenth and fourteenth centuries to describe the fireplace as a whole. Several words were used at this time for the fireplace and smoke stack — for example, fumeral, femeras and tuel. The different words reflected the various languages of the Normans and Saxons.

Chimney-stack is a corruption of the term "chimney stalk", which meant just the part of the chimney that rose above the roof. Today a chimney-stack is considered to be the whole of the shaft that leads from the fireplace to the chimney-pot. The *chimney-pot*, the clay pot inserted at the opening of the stack, has regional names: for example, chimney "can" in Scotland, and in South West England it is known as the chimney "tun".

Norman castles built from the eleventh century had stone shafts leading from the fireplace, situated by the stone wall, to wall vents, which expelled the smoke. By the thirteenth century a few rich homes had circular stone chimney-stacks. The Normans favoured stone as a building material and used it wherever possible. Stone chimney-stacks were a feature popular in Europe and the Normans built them in Britain, although the Saxon community continued to use the "louvre" and open hearth.

Inside the medieval timber-framed house, smoke was led to the smoke hole by means of a funnel-shaped *hood*, made of wattle and daub. The hood was suspended over the hearth or, to give it better support by the walls, the hearth could be set to one side of the room, not centrally. Because of the risk of catching the wall alight, the fire could not be set against a wooden-framed wall without some protection for the wall. This was provided in better homes by a fireback or *reredos*, a false wall made of clay or stone, placed between the hearth and the timber walls.

The hood and reredos were the origins of the modern chimney-stack and were very popular by the fourteenth century. The fire risk to timber houses was still great, even

▲
78   A stone shaft for the smoke to escape.

with a reredos, and so bye-laws were introduced in London, prohibiting a reredos from being placed near any inflammable walls.

79   A wattle and daub hood over a hearth.
▼

39

The need for a fireproof smoke outlet was answered in the fifteenth century by the brick chimney-stack. Although still expensive, brick was becoming more widely available. Timber-framed houses were still the most commonly constructed homes, but a brick chimney-stack could be added externally to existing buildings or could be built onto the gable-end walls of new houses. Adding brick stacks to timber houses could be done in several ways. Some small timber homes could have an internal stack built against the wall of the *cross passage*, that is the corridor that divided the building into two parts, at one time for animals and for human occupants. The animal section of the house was now more often used as a store room and the animals were kept in outbuildings. The chimney-stack built internally would emerge from the roof at the ridge, and this was called an *axial chimney*.

The large medieval hall was renovated by having a stack built on the site of the central fireplace, rising up through the centre of the roof ridge. This stack supported beams of wood which divided the hall, giving an upper floor and ground floor. These could also be divided, so that there were two upper rooms, heated by the stack, and two lower rooms, each with a fireplace sharing the central stack.

Brick chimney-stacks were in great demand in the fifteenth century and were constructed with pride. Even some stone-walled houses, that would usually have had stone stacks, followed fashion and had an ornamental brick stack added to them. The stack above the roof was built with moulded bricks in elaborate styles. The brickmakers acquired their skills from Holland, but only in Britain did the chimney-stack become very ornate, with twists and spirals. The most decorative stacks were constructed in Henry VIII's reign.

The fireplaces now were enclosed; the open hearth remained only in the poorest homes. Strong timbers framed the large fireplace, and the timber lintel, the horizontal beam over the fireplace, was often

▲
80   A brick chimney stack at the gable end of a timber-framed house.

richly carved in wealthy homes into a fine *mantelpiece*. In the yeoman's home, bread ovens were added to one side of the hearth. Bars were inserted across the inside of the stack, to take hooks for hanging cooking pots and spits on which to roast meat. The hearth was large enough to seat people close to the fire, and ledges in the hearth wall were made to take a *salt box*, to keep the precious salt dry.

Salt was used to preserve meat and some vegetables, for use during the winter months. Without it, people would have no winter

81   Tudor chimney stacks.
▼

82 An inglenook fireplace.

83 A decorated fireback.

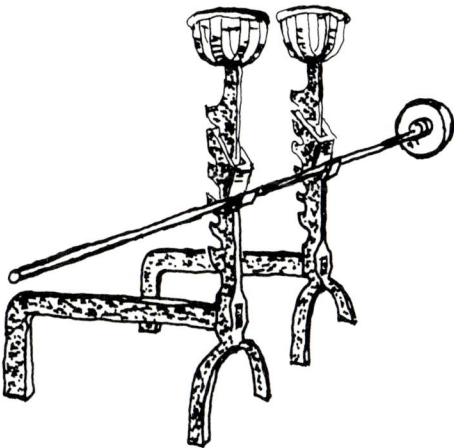

84 Firedogs.

meat, as only a few breeding animals were kept after the autumn harvest, when all surplus animals were killed. This was because the farmers could not grow enough hay for winter feed and the growing of root vegetables to feed stock had not been considered. It was not until the seventeenth century, when Jethro Tull introduced crop rotation, that root crops like turnips were grown, to feed farm animals throughout the winter, and salt meat became less popular.

An alternative to salting meat was to "cure" it, by hanging it in smoke. Sometimes, part of the flue, that is the inside of the stack, was divided off to make an area where bacon could be made by curing pork.

The large Tudor fireplace, often known as the *inglenook* fireplace, was the centre of family life for the majority of people. The fireplace was in continuous use and the bricks or stone at the back of the hearth needed protection from the heat. *Firebacks* — metal plates — were made and fixed to the back wall of the fireplace. Wealthier homes had ornate firebacks. Designs such as family crests were shaped in damp sand moulds; liquid iron was then poured into the mould and so the sheet of iron was produced, to be secured to the back of the fireplace.

The large log-burning hearths needed a metal grid and frame to support the fire, and *firedogs* came into being, some very handsome in design.

Coal had been used as fuel from ancient times. The Romans mined it, but coal found near the surface or picked up from the seashore was probably the main source in Britain, at first. People living near coal-producing areas would have used it readily, but its use in non-coal areas would have relied on water transport, as travelling overland was not easy before the eighteenth century and coal would have been expensive. London breweries and bakeries used *sea-coal* — coal transported by sea — from the end of the thirteenth century, when they were banned from burning straw, but it was not until the seventeenth century that many

41

people could afford to burn coal in their homes.

Coal was found to burn best if placed in an iron basket, supported by four legs — these were called *grates*. Chimney-stacks did not have to be so large for coal-burning fires, as smaller amounts of coal produce the same heat as a large log fire, and coal burns more slowly than wood. Chimney-stacks were also reduced in width for coal-burning fireplaces, as the volume of smoke was less; but bends in the stack were introduced, to improve the *updraught*, the current of air and smoke needed to remove the unpleasant coal smoke.

In 1662, King Charles II levied a tax on fireplaces or hearths, at ten pence a hearth, and this affected every home except the very small cottages. The tax lasted for more than twenty-five years and was very unpopular. It was eventually removed by William III.

It was the fashion to place the stack centrally in the home and to place it at an angle to the roof ridge. Several stacks, serving several rooms, might be placed in a row at an angle, giving a distinctive appearance to the seventeenth-century house.

Strict laws on the construction of flues were introduced in 1709 and 1764, which forbade, for example, timber to be nearer than twelve centimetres to the fireplace. Plaster was used to cover the offending exposed wood.

85   Stacks at an angle to the roof ridge, seventeenth century.

▼

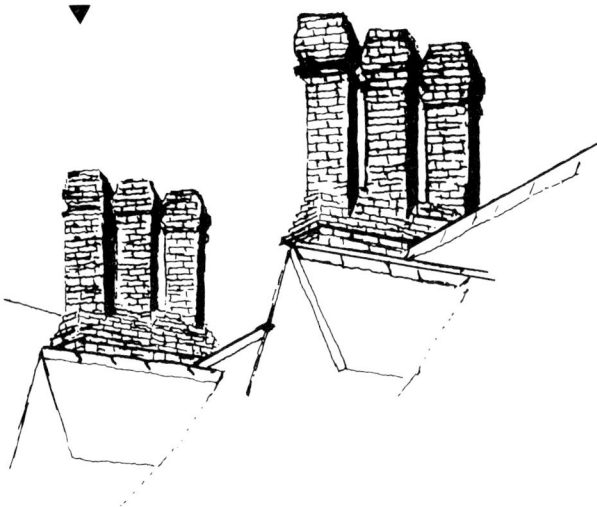

Chimney Sweeping

The large, straight, Tudor chimney-stacks could easily be swept by their owners. A holly bush or gorze bush, weighted with a stone tied on with string, was lowered or dropped down the chimney shaft. Soot was thus scraped off the sides, by the thorns, and fell with a rush into the hearth. This process could be repeated until, looking up the chimney-stack from the fireplace, you could see a clean stack and sky.

The narrower, winding stacks, built for coal-burning grates, needed cleaning more frequently than log-burning hearths, and the traditional holly bush and stone sweeping method was not practical in the seventeenth century. It was from this time that the practice started of employing children to sweep the inside of the stack with hand brushes. The children, mainly boys, though girl sweeps were sometimes used, were apprenticed to master sweeps, from the age of six years. They were often subjected to cruel persuasion to make them climb the stacks, frequently still hot from recent fires in the hearth. Because of long exposure and contact with the soot, they could also contract a sweep's cancer.

In 1826 a mechanical device for chimney cleaning was devised — the *scandiscope* — which was the original telescopic sweep's brush. It took the form of a large disc-like brush, attached to a short rod, to which other short rods could be attached as the brush was pushed up the chimney. The jointed rods could bend with the shape of the stack, and the brush could be withdrawn, when the chimney had been swept, by releasing the sections of rod one at a time.

The Society for the Abolition of Chimney Sweeping by small boys recommended the use of the scandiscope, but even with the support of the society's royal patron, George IV, it did not stop the employment of child sweeps.

Laws passed in 1840 and 1864 improved the chimney sweep's life, but it was not until 1875 that the employment of child sweeps was forbidden. No one under the age of twenty-one was allowed to climb flues, and apprentices were not to be employed below the age of sixteen years. Master sweeps also had to be licensed for a fee of 2/6d (12½ pence). Chimneys from then on were swept with brushes and jointed canes, and during the second half of the twentieth century chimney sweeps have used vacuum cleaners as well as brushes, to remove soot.

Chimney-Pots

Although clay chimney-pots had been made in medieval times, it was not until the eighteenth century that their use became widespread. The new fuel, coal, produced smoke that was very unpleasant when blown back down the flues into the house, by adverse winds. Many experiments were done and there was much discussion as to the best arrangement of bends in the stack and shapes of pots, to try to improve the situation. The popular shapes for chimney-pots in the eighteenth century were either square or cylindrical, and there were also some experimental horned and spouted versions which tried to improve smoke dispersal.

Early eighteenth-century pots were hand-made by potters using a wheel, and were made in brickyards. The marks of the potter's

86 Simple hand-made chimney-pots, early eighteenth century.

▼

▲

87 Regency "orange" chimney-pots from the end of the eighteenth century.

▲

88 A tallboy.

wheel and hands can be seen on these old pots, which were plain in appearance. Sometimes a band of white glaze was placed around the upper part, or bands of pattern were sketched in by hand on the wet clay, before the pot was fired. The tallest chimney-pot could only be the length of the potter's arm, which had to reach down inside the wet clay pot to shape it. If a "tallboy" was required, that is, a pot one metre or more in height, then two pots were joined together by the potter, while the clay was still wet. Tall chimney-pots could be used in place of high brick stacks, to carry smoke over the roof tops. Houses that had burnt wood, but had changed to coal, sometimes added tallboys to their stacks to improve the updraught. It was thought that, by restricting the exit of the stack, the smoke would be driven out more efficiently.

43

89 Stacks built into the gable-end walls of a late eighteenth-century house.

The fashionable position for eighteenth-century stacks was the gable-end walls, to enhance the symmetry of the house. A cream-coloured, square chimney-pot was favoured, to harmonize with white stucco walls.

By the nineteenth century, the building of terrace and semi-detached houses for the industrial towns brought a boom in chimney-pot making. Pots were now made in moulds, to help keep up with demand.

Stacks serving several rooms in the house terminated on the roof in clusters of pots, in rows of twos, fours or eights, as required. Regional styles in pots were, and still are, noticeable, although improved transport meant that pots made in one area were used in places all over the country, according to architects' and builders' desires. For example, the cream-coloured, square tulip top, seen on rows of Durham miners' houses, can also be seen in Southern England. Other shapes of chimney-pot to be looked for, apart from cylinders of varying heights and square pots, are the H and half-H, louvres and octagonals. These can be decorated at the top with spikes, crenellations, tulip shapes and moulded rings. *Caps*, like inverted saucers, or hoods, like saddles, can be placed just above the smoke hole. Chimney-pots can be decorated with raised patterns and rings, and have pieces cut out of the side to make spouts or slits for louvres in various numbers. A walk through the Victorian part of a brick-built town will reveal many intriguing chimney-pot shapes, such as the jelly mould with a spiked crown, described in a catalogue at the turn of this century simply as a smoke cure!

Cowls

Chimney *cowls* or hoods are metallic chimney-pots, which were devised during the early twentieth century to stop down-draughts. The main feature of cowls is that they revolve or move with the wind, so positioning their openings to give the best dispersal of smoke, in any wind direction. However, without regular attention, the moving parts become fixed and their purpose is lost. One of the more interesting designs is the lobster-back and another is the helmet-shaped cowl, known in Scotland as the "granny".

90

a tulip top	f curved roll
b moulded roll	g hooded horn
c louvre	h plain roll taper
d plain square	i squared, spiked panel
e octagonal	

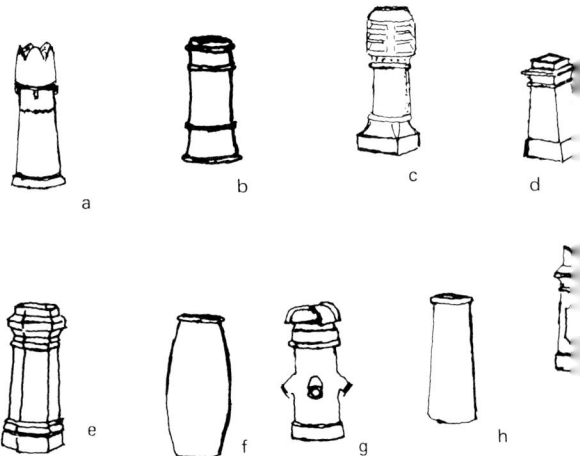

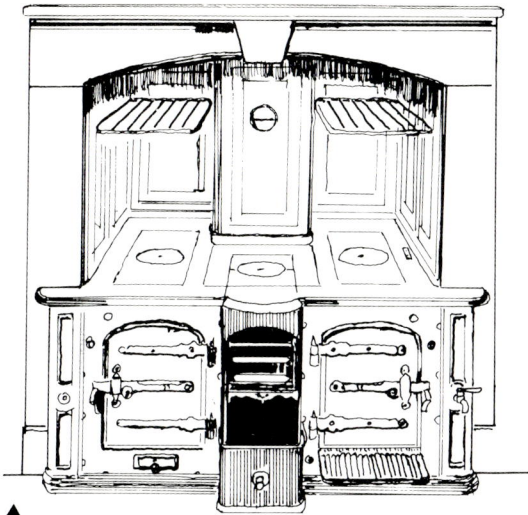

▲
91 A Victorian kitchen range.

▲
92 Gas flues.

Grates and Fireplaces

Victorian builders, besides indulging in multiple chimney-stacks and pots, also tried to copy the ornate brick stacks of Tudor times, though the results were not quite the same. In the Victorian living room were small cast-iron grates surrounded by highly adorned frames, with a shelf, made of wood or marble, called a mantelpiece, that created the focal point in the better homes. In the kitchen, the fire was enclosed in a large iron box-like structure called a *range*, with an oven on one side of the fire and a boiler for heating water on the other side. As in Tudor times, the fireplace in the kitchen, in the form of the iron range, was the social centre of the poorer family.

Coal-burning grates in all the main rooms of the house were still a feature of the twentieth-century home until after the Second World War. Living room fireplaces had simpler mantelpieces than in Victorian times and the fireplace surround was tiled. Kitchen fires were no longer needed to cook with, as gas and electric cookers were introduced, and so the fire was enclosed in a small *boiler* and used to heat water. Hot water on tap for baths and washing was a new luxury.

Modern Heating

From the middle of the twentieth century alternative means of heating the home became dominant. Gas, oil or electric *central heating* are features of modern homes. Gas- and oil-burning boilers heat water that circulates to radiators in the home, and only a simple stack, terminated by a small, vertically louvred pot, is needed to extract the fumes. The all-electric house requires no chimney-stack, as it has no fireplace, although ventilators are often inserted into the roof ridge, to circulate air in the roof space or loft. Open coal fires still form a useful part of the domestic heating systems of the country, and smokeless fuels derived from coal are used to fuel boilers for hot water central heating.

The presence of chimney-stacks in future houses is uncertain, and will depend on which fuel becomes the most economical to use. The age of the multi-stack and rows of chimney-pots which dominated the Victorian skyline seems unlikely ever to return, although advertisements can still be found, explaining the virtues of the latest device for curing smoky chimneys! Chimney-pots are now collectors' items.

6
Inside the Home,
1000~1650 AD

Rooms

Looking at the outside of houses only gives a general idea of the inside appearance — the arrangement of rooms, their contents and decoration. Perhaps the curiosity aroused by external appearances has been a factor that has made visits to stately homes so popular today. There are fewer opportunities to see inside humbler dwellings, but open air museums, where reconstructed old houses may be seen, are becoming more numerous and are well worth visiting. Tudor homes seen in a village or a museum seem familiar in their house structure, but inside they would have been very different from what we know. Modern technology has brought a vast improvement in home comforts. For this we must thank electricity and modern plumbing!

The basic requirement of a home is that it should provide shelter. In this shelter safety is found, from the climate and intruders, so that a family might sleep and eat in peace

and have security for themselves and their possessions. The shelter also provides a base from which to earn a living. With the addition of barns, a farmer can work from home, as he does today. In the past, craftsmen, such as weavers and blacksmiths, used the rooms of the home to work in, or added an out-building. Few people work from home today, but before the Industrial Revolution it was the normal thing to do.

In early medieval times the one-room house was the most common, and it provided all the family's needs. The family's most valuable animal was also kept under the same roof, at one end of the room, separated from the family by a wicker partition. A central fire provided heat for warmth and cooking.

The Saxon chief or Norman baron had a larger home, built on the *hall house* style. Here the soldiers, servants and family lived, in a large hall open to the roof rafters, where smoke drifted from the central hearth. The nobleman's family ate at one end of the hall, apart from the rest of the household. At this end of the hall, a wattle and daub screen or a stone rubble wall was constructed, to make a separate room, called the *solar*, for the nobleman's family to retire to. The rest slept in the main hall. The solar was sometimes on first-floor level, with a storeroom below, and was reached by an outside staircase. The Normans favoured this style of manor house.

93 Plan of a Saxon hall.

▼

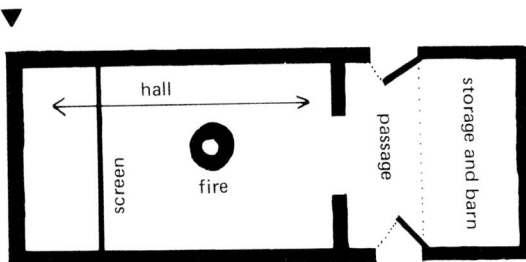

hall

screen

fire

passage

storage and barn

In the Saxon hall, at the opposite end to the solar, there would be a barn area, separated from the hall by a cross passage. Here the valuable oxen could be stabled.

The space between a pair of crucks, which formed the frame for the great Saxon hall, was called a *bay*, as described in Chapter 1 (page 7). It was about sixteen feet or five metres long and was the space needed to stable four oxen side by side. The length of the bay — sixteen feet — became the length in which land was measured, variably called a rod, pole or perch. Grain was also measured by the amount a bay could hold and houses were taxed by the number of bays in the length of the house. Kitchens, stables and storerooms were built in a courtyard around the hall or manor house.

The *long house* plan, as the hall house style was also called, persisted until the seventeenth century, as it proved very adaptable for large or small homes, and improvements and additions could easily be made, to increase the house size. Extra space could be provided by *extending* the roof to make an aisle or gallery room along one or both sides of the cruck frame. The extension was called an *outshut* or *outshot*. This form of additional space did not increase the house tax, whereas an extra bay added to the length of the house did. Farmers used the cross passage to thresh their grain and, as this passage was the main entrance to the house, so arose the modern word *threshold*, meaning the entrance-step to a house.

By later medieval times, the central hearth was not so popular and it was moved to the wall of the cross passage. Hoods were built over the hearth, or chimney-stacks were constructed. Animals were given their own barns, and the animal bay on the other side of the cross passage became a kitchen or buttery. Tall halls were divided, to give an upper floor, for use as bedrooms and storage areas. These were reached by ladders or simple stairs. Even the poorer families now had two ground-floor rooms, plus bedrooms above, reached by stairs from the main living room. One ground-floor room was used as a living room-combined-kitchen, where the fireplace was situated, with perhaps an oven built beside it, and the second room became the parlour. Here the ladies could withdraw, to spin, weave or sew.

Early medieval towns were small, and walled for protection. The houses of wood were single-roomed, with the gable-end facing the street. There was a yard at the back and perhaps a stable. As town populations increased, there was little land available for horizontal extensions, which country homes could enjoy, and so vertical expansion took place. Box-framed houses were favoured for town houses and these could be heightened by placing beams of wood across the lower room's ceiling, so that they extended a little out over the street. These beams then took the weight of the room above and up to four or five storeys could be added in this way. Thus the jetty house evolved. A room could also be excavated below the ground-floor room, to make a cellar.

94   A cruck house with outshut.
▼

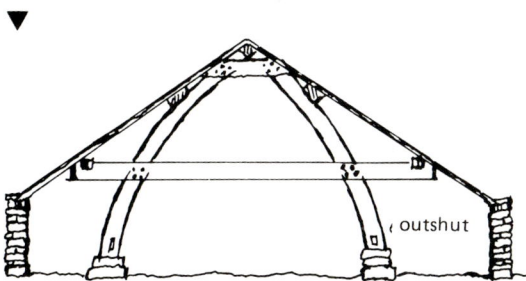

95   Plan of a long house, modified.
▼

47

Many town houses were owned by traders, and cellars became their shops, with steps leading up to the street for customers' use. Workshops occupied the back of the shop. These cellar shops were called *taverns* and, in time, traders in wine became especially associated with taverns; hence the modern use of the word to mean a "drinking house" or public house.

Trade was also carried on from stalls; boards were fixed to the walls of buildings by the road, to make a table-top on which goods could be displayed. At night, the stall could be folded back to the wall and secured. Ground-floor rooms in town houses were also used as shops and they used horizontally hinged window shutters, which could be lowered and supported, to make a counter. At night, this too could be folded back against the window, which it now secured.

Shops selling similar goods tended to trade in the same street and street names today can still be found illustrating this custom; for example, Leather Lane, Baker Street, Pudding Lane.

Medieval towns had very narrow, crowded streets and, as the jetties increased, these streets became gloomier. By the fifteenth century a typical town house might consist of a cellar, for storage purposes, a ground-floor shop and workroom, where apprentices and servants lived, a first-floor room where the owner's family lived, a second-floor solar or bedroom, and a garret room in the roof for servants' bedrooms. Apprentices slept in the shop. A kitchen and stable would be built in a back yard, where an *earth closet*, or lavatory, *might* be provided. Terraced town houses in London had to have thick stone walls dividing the houses from each other (*party walls*) from the twelfth century, and it was against the stone wall that fires were lit on the ground-floor hearth. Smoke escaped through a hole in the ceiling and if there were rooms above, false walls or wattle screens were built beside the stone party wall to provide a space for the smoke to escape directly to the roof louvre. At night, the fire had to be put out. The introduction into these homes of the brick chimney-stack was a great improvement and enabled hearths to be made on upper floors.

In Northern Britain the *Bastle house* was built, to protect the family from raiders in the unsettled border areas of Northumberland and Scotland. The Bastle house was built of stone, with a ground-floor area where cattle could be kept and an upper floor where the family lived. The upper floor was reached by an internal ladder or external stone flight of stairs. The Bastle house had few windows and the chimney was built at the gable-end of the building. The house was like a miniature fortress and reflected troubled times.

96   Plan of a two-roomed house.
▼

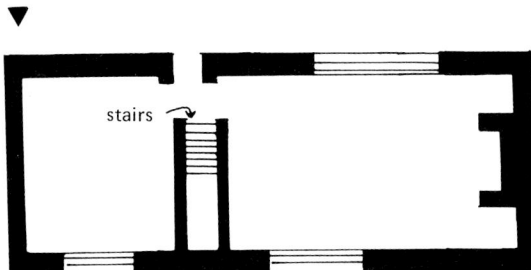

stairs

97   Cross-section of a medieval town house, showing the fireplace and smoke screens.
▼

48

By the sixteenth century, home improvements increased rapidly. Brick chimneys and glass windows were being included in the homes of rich merchants and farmers. The yeoman, as these men were called, improved his hall house by making the barn in the house into a kitchen; the great hall became a general living room; and the solar a parlour or sitting room. The cross passage and threshing floor became the hallway to the main door. The upper part of the building had a floor inserted, to make bedrooms, which were reached by a staircase built next to the chimney-stack, to give it support.

Stairs

The simplest way to reach an upper floor, loft or roof space is to use a ladder. The Saxons made a ladder by splitting a log into four, each quarter making a step, and these steps were secured by wooden pegs to two long lengths of wood, so forming a ladder. This could be secured by metal hooks to the entrance hole leading to the upper rooms. The stone buildings of the Normans had stairways made of stone slabs in a single flight, or a spiral stairway where the slabs were inserted at one end into the two walls of a corner and overlapped each other at the centre of the spiral to make a supporting shaft. This gave a steep flight of stairs and is a form of construction known today as a geometrical staircase.

By Tudor times home improvements included the stairs, and the *newel* and *dog leg* styles were popular. However, these took up quite a lot of space. If the yeoman's hall house was being renovated, the central chimney-stack could be used as a support, instead of a newel post. A newel staircase was like a broad spiral staircase. The dog leg style could take up part of the cross passage and consisted of a straight flight of stairs leading to a landing, where a half turn led to a second flight, which led to the upper floor. Large houses might have a *well* style of stairway, which involved

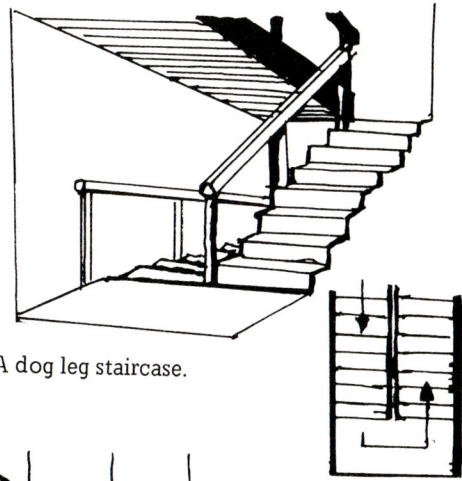

98a A dog leg staircase.

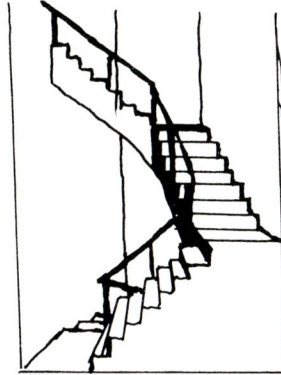

◀ 98b A well staircase.

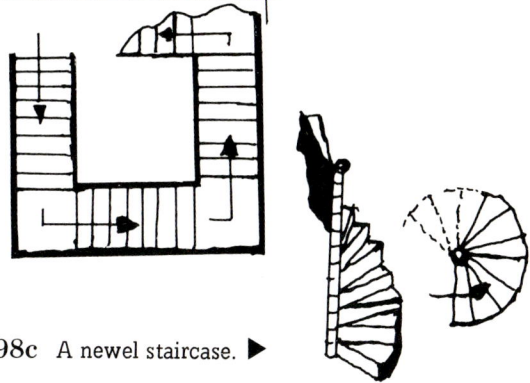

98c A newel staircase. ▶

two landings and three flights of straight stairs which enclosed a space or well. These staircases, although fixed, were not often framed or encased in wood panels, although handrails were included. An extension to the house was needed — a staircase wing — if the original house was not large enough to take a new stairway, and this would be built onto the back of the house. Very poor houses kept their ladders, and stone houses still used the simple Norman style of staircase.

Floors

The beaten earth floor was the simplest Saxon floor and this was usually strewn with rushes, straw or bracken. Stone *flags* were used on floors, where stone was available, as were cobbles and slate. Stone flags were often limewashed in the form of a pattern around the edge of the floor, to make a border, and the rest of the floor was strewn with sand. A mixture of ox blood and ashes laid evenly over an earth floor gave a flat, hard surface and was popular in the sixteenth century. However, flagstones for kitchen floors were an improvement which the yeomen tried to include, although straw-strewn earth floors persisted till the seventeenth century. Upper rooms had rough floor-boards with plaster-filled cracks.

Walls

The Saxons plastered the wattle walls of their homes, mainly to keep out draughts and protect the wood and twigs from fire. However, they also appreciated colour and patterns and so decorated the plaster. Colours would be added to the basic white limewash, and blue and yellow were popular. Blue was obtained from the liverwort plants and yellow ochre was made by burning together hydrate oxide of iron and clay. The walls of stone houses were also limewashed and in Northern Britain the *witch-worm* pattern was popular. This was a frieze design painted at the join of the wall and ceiling, consisting of a wavy line with spots placed in the curves of the waves. It seems to reflect a wickerwork pattern and was popular in bedrooms. Green ceilings were also favoured, the green obtained by adding sulphate of iron to limewash. Stencils were used to make repeating patterns on the walls, perhaps of

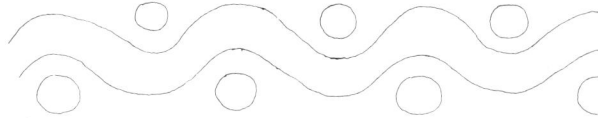

▲
99   Witch-worm pattern.

leaves, and murals depicting hunting scenes might be painted on the walls of better homes. Woven tapestries, often illustrating battle scenes, were hung on the walls of the rich man's home and these gave insulation as well as colourful decoration. Banners and cloth drapery also adorned the richer home. Painted cloths were the poorer version of the woven tapestries and usually depicted biblical scenes. The painted cloths were stretched over a wooden frame and hung from the wall.

By the late fifteenth century curtains were hung over doorways to prevent draughts, and wood-panelled walls were introduced. Wood panels were called *wainscot*, from an old Dutch word meaning "wall board", and became very elaborately carved by the end of the Tudor period. Wainscot today has lost its original grand meaning and popularly refers to the skirting board, the narrow board that runs along the foot of an internal wall to prevent the wall plaster from being knocked. In timber-framed homes, even the shutters and exposed timbers were brightly coloured in medieval times.

Wallpaper was originally made in China and the idea came to England via Flemish traders. The earliest record of English wallpaper being made was in the early sixteenth century. The paper was made from old shredded rags — *flock paper* — and was decorated in the same way and used like the painted cloths. Biblical scenes might be painted on the paper, or it could be painted to look like material. Wallpaper was very expensive at this time.

7
Inside the Home, 1650~1980 AD

The seventeenth century brought changes in the hall house or long house plan. Brick-built houses were increasing in number, and privacy and comfort were sought in the home. Timber-framed houses bore the weight of the roof on the posts which formed the frame, but houses built of brick had the weight of the roof spread over the whole walls. Walls dividing the house into rooms eased the weight on the outer walls. Houses were built, two rooms deep, with a double-span roof. In richer homes this could be seen as a "double fronted" house, with two rooms in the front, used as a parlour and dining room, on either side of a central hallway, and two rooms at the rear, used as a kitchen and general living room. In the hallway a staircase led to the upper rooms, which might be four bedrooms. Attic rooms were made in the roof, with dormer windows providing daylight.

Smaller homes would consist of two rooms downstairs, a parlour and a kitchen-combined-living room, and two bedrooms — a "two up, two down" style, often built as semi-detached or terraced houses. Because hallways and passageways were central in the building, *fanlights* over front doorways were introduced to provide daylight. Later in the eighteenth century panels were removed from the upper part of the door and replaced with glass to give even more light to the hallway. Windows in upstairs

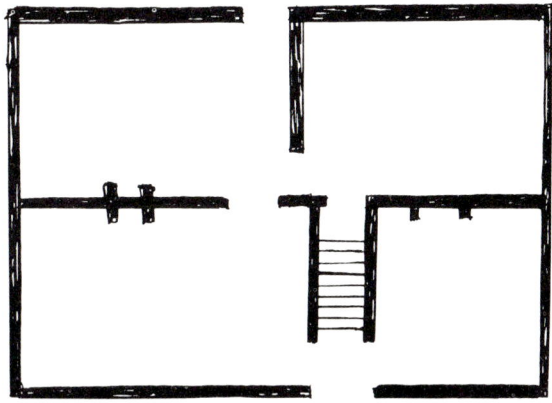

100   Plan of a brick square-plan house.

landing walls, over the front door, became popular and the Regency trellised balcony in front of this landing window, was a distinctive feature of the period. The roof space was now commonly used for attic bedrooms, and dormer windows, typically with hipped roofs, provided light. Elegant terraced town houses, sometimes two or three storeys high, were the pride of the Georgian period.

However, as the Industrial Revolution increased its influence, more and more people left the countryside to find work in towns and were housed in poorly built terraces which soon became slums. These homes consisted of two rooms up and two rooms down, with a staircase leading from the living room

101 A copper for heating water for washing clothes.

to the upper rooms and one leading down to the cellar from the kitchen. Front doors opened directly from the living room onto the street outside. These terraces were often built "back to back"; that is, the back wall of the house, as well as the two side walls, was shared by neighbours. A communal earth closet, emptied perhaps weekly in some areas, or monthly in others, by the "night soil man", was shared by many families. Many elegant Georgian town houses were turned into flats to cope with the increase in town populations by the early nineteenth century and soon added to the slums.

During the Victorian era better homes were built in the suburbs of towns for the middle-income families. Semi-detached and terraced villas, with ground-floor bay windows, were typical. The house could be three or four rooms deep, with a passage leading to each room from a front door, now half panelled in obscure glass. The front room would be the parlour, the second room a sitting room or dining room, then a kitchen with a coal-burning range for cooking, and a scullery. The scullery was a small room, added to the back of the house, containing the only tap for cold water, and where the washing-up was done in a stone sink. This emptied by a pipe into a soakaway. Also in the scullery was a "*copper*" for boiling the clothes on wash day and once a year for boiling the Christmas pudding! The copper was a large metal tub set in a brick frame, which was plastered over. There was a space below the tub where a coal fire could be lit, and a chimney led out of the back. As gas became available for domestic use, gas-fired coppers, as well as cookers, replaced the coal range and copper.

Upstairs were the bedrooms and attic, but no bathroom. It was not until the late nineteenth century that rooms for baths were provided in ordinary homes or it became popular to turn small bedrooms into bathrooms, in older houses. Bathing had not been considered a healthy thing to do, very often.

Metal baths or *hip baths* were used for the occasional bath and these were placed in the bedroom in better homes. They were then laboriously filled with water, brought from the communal pump and heated on the coal range, and afterwards emptied by the maids. In poorer homes miners probably bathed more regularly than anyone else in the early nineteenth century. The metal bath was placed in front of the kitchen range and was filled with water heated by the boiler, which was to one side of the range fire, opposite to the oven. After use, the metal bath was often hung on a nail on the door of the coal shed or the back wall of the house.

102 A hip bath.

Large basins and jugs of cold water on a stand in the bedroom provided the means of daily personal washing in ordinary homes, or faces and hands were washed under the pump in the court yards. The only lavatory arrangements inside the home were the chamber pot or, in richer homes, the *commode*. This was a chair with a removable seat, that covered a chamber pot below it. After use, it had to be cleaned by the maids.

Sanitation had been poor for centuries and sanitary conditions were becoming intolerable in the crowded towns of the early nineteenth century. Cesspits could not cope with the sewage; ditches and rivers were heavily polluted. Earth closets in towns were cleaned at night by the "scavenger" or "night soil man". They might be cleaned regularly once a week in good areas, but only three or four times a year in slum areas. The sewage was piled onto carts and sold as manure, to fertilize the land. The polluted water in streams and ditches seeped into wells which were used for drinking water. Communal pumps, which brought the water to the surface, were the main source of drinking water for centuries, although water carriers would sell water, brought from country streams, to towns-people, at a high price. Only a few privileged people were allowed to pipe water from the communal supply, and this was in thin pipes, called *quills*, which provided a mere trickle of water on certain days of the week only. Pumps were needed to improve the supply, but were not efficiently provided till the latter part of the nineteenth century. Attempts were made to pipe water to individual homes from the seventeenth century, but these were not very successful. In the middle of the nineteenth century there was a serious outbreak of cholera in London, a disease that often occurred because of contaminated water. The government at last took action, in a series of Public Health Acts, which enabled local government to clear away slums, put in proper sewerage drains and pipe clean water to homes.

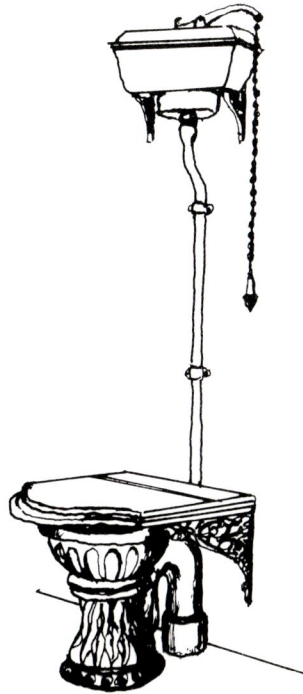

▲
103 A lavatory with overhead cistern.

By the end of the nineteenth century piped water began regularly to be installed in homes (one tap per house in the scullery or kitchen at first), and main drainage pipes were provided to carry away sewage and dirty water. The opportunity was now provided for bathrooms, as we know them, to be included in newly built homes. It was not until after the First World War (1914-1918), however, that bathrooms were considered an essential part of the home. Lavatories were still installed in outbuildings, but they could now be flushed clean with water piped to an overhead cistern. By the time the Second World War began in 1939, homes for ordinary people were being built with lavatories inside the home, often included with the now essential bathroom. Coke-burning stoves provided hot water to both kitchen and bathroom taps, which was a welcome luxury.

The bathroom in the average modern home may now include shower units and bidets as well as baths and wash basins.

There may also be two or more lavatories situated in their own rooms, which may have a hand basin too. However, the sanitation arrangements of the past are still with us in Britain, in a few rural areas.

Stairs

Stairways had elaborately carved wooden frames and handrails from the Tudor period into the eighteenth century, when stairs began to be encased with panels. A cupboard was made under the staircase, and was often the only one in a small home. When chimneys were placed at the gable-ends of the eighteenth-century house, to enhance its symmetry, so conforming to fashion, this enabled the staircase to become a feature in the centre of the larger house, in a hallway opposite the main door. In rich homes wrought-iron handrails and ballustrades were popular.

The position of the staircase has remained close to the main entrance of the house, although modifications in its shape occur, according to the type of house. The straight flight of narrow stairs is common in many terraced houses, but the newel and dog leg styles can be found in larger homes. Modern staircases in some instances have been left uncased again, as in the "open plan" style, and even the spiral staircase is familiar once more.

Floors

Where cellars were built under a house, a boarded ground-room floor was naturally provided, and gradually all ground floors were boarded. The parlour floor was the first to be improved in this manner. Kitchens had stone flag floors and, in the early eighteenth century, brick floors were made in hallways. By the late eighteenth century polished wooden floors, with some carpet or rugs over them, were usual. Before this time,

carpets were very expensive, mainly being imported from Eastern countries, but with the coming of the industrial age, that is, from the late eighteenth century, carpets were made in Britain. By the mid-nineteenth century tiles and flagstones might cover hall floors and by the end of the century *linoleum* was being made and was a popular floor covering. Rugs made from rags, woven onto a hessian backing, are a well-known floor mat in the North of England. The *hooky* mat and the *proggy* mat were made from late Victorian times, and the tradition still carries on. The difference between the two mats is in the way the pieces of rag are woven into the hessian.

Stair carpet came into general use during the nineteenth century, depending, of course, on the family income. Modern homes are now well-carpeted, synthetic fibres making a cheaper carpet than traditional wool. Plastic-based floor covering replaces linoleum, and ceramic tiles are popular for bathroom and kitchen floors, and walls.

Walls and Ceilings

Plaster and wainscot were still the main covering for walls in the late seventeenth and early eighteenth centuries. In richer homes, only the lower part of the wall might be panelled; the upper half would be plastered and decorated with painted plaster mouldings — *stucco*.

By the mid-eighteenth century woodblock hand-printed wallpapers became available from English wallpaper makers, although the Eastern wallpapers were still popular in rich homes. As wallpaper increased in popularity, wood panelling declined. Early wallpapers were made in short lengths which were stuck to a canvas backing and mounted onto a wooden frame, to make a panel. The panel was then attached to the wall by wooden pegs. The effect was reminiscent of tapestry hangings. Wallpaper was not made in continuous long strips until

104　Plaster decoration of cornices and walls.

the mid-nineteenth century, when it was machine-printed and rapidly became the dominant wall covering.

The wall of the typical Victorian home was divided into several horizontal layers. An area between the ceiling and the picture rail was the *frieze*, about half a metre deep. From the picture rail to the *dado* was wall-papered, and the dado was the wood panelling which covered the lower metre of the wall. The walls of very poor homes were still only plastered and colour-washed.

Ceilings were plastered and painted throughout the period of the brick house, but relief mouldings were used to decorate the cornices and central lighting area of the ceiling, according to the owner's income. By the late Victorian period, cornices with plaster-relief leaves and fruits and a central circle reflecting the cornice were typical.

Twentieth-century ceilings became much simpler, and plain white emulsioned ceilings are popular today. Walls also became simpler and picture rails became rare by the mid-twentieth century. Wallpaper friezes — a narrow strip of paper pasted between the ceiling and the wallpaper — became popular. Heavy wallpaper, *lincrusta*, sometimes took the place of the lower wood panelling of the walls, popular a century before. For modern walls there is a variety of wall coverings to choose from, but wallpaper and emulsion paint are still the main choice.

8
The Whole House

During the past one thousand years social, economic and technical changes have altered the life style of man, and his home has been adapted to meet his present needs. If people have changed, however, there are still examples of houses that have altered little in appearance for centuries. They linger into the twentieth century, not ghosts, but survivors from the past.

To survive, of course, an old building has to have been originally well-built, in durable materials, and to have been cared for and restored, when needed, in the style of its construction. Old houses often survive as part of newer homes that have been built onto them. Or they have been adapted and altered to suit the requirements and fashions of a new generation of occupiers. A modern house, like modern man, reflects its ancestry, but meets modern standards and needs.

To date a whole building from external appearance is difficult. Even new, modern houses are soon personalized by their owners, who, if they are fashion-conscious, may readily change doors and windows to suit a popular fancy. Therefore, one has to be a detective to recognize what is the basic style and age of the house and what has been altered, added or renewed. Doors and windows easily deteriorate and are most commonly replaced and, if the replacements are not in the original style of the house, then the house detective should recognize the difference. Walls and roofs are a better guide to the age of the house, but even these can be deceiving. Claddings and even false walls can be added to the front of a house, for example, to disguise a timber-framed house as an elegant Georgian home. Although the walls may be clad and doors and windows changed to give the eighteenth-century "look", if the house were surmounted by a gabled, steep sloping roof, this would be uncharacteristic and suggest an original thatched roof of an earlier time. People sometimes only alter the front of their homes and ignore the back, and so this is where the detective will find evidence of the real age and structure of the house.

The feature that has the oldest style will probably yield the original date of that part of the building. However, because very old houses are admired by many people, false features may be added to age a building. The Georgian style of house has always been admired, especially in the last century. Today, timber-framed buildings are admired and the "mock Tudor" house can be seen. Planks of wood are nailed to white plastered walls, to imitate posts and pans, but if the timbers are examined, the carpentry will reveal their newness. Jointings, the thickness of the wood and fastenings, which would be wooden pegs in the Tudor period, would indicate the truth. To whiten plaster walls and paint the posts black does not produce a timber-framed house as it would have looked in Tudor times. Brown oak beams and creamy coloured plaster, decorated with colourful wall paintings, would be more authentic.

If a house can be entered and the rafters in the roof examined, this could give a very accurate date to the house. The carpenters' methods of jointing timbers, and the arrangement of supporting beams, are characteristic for given periods. The internal rafters and pitch and shape of the roof are, therefore, a good indicator of its period, if original.

Walls made of brick can also be a useful guide to the walls' age — look at the size and colour of the bricks and whether they are hand- or machine-made, as revealed by surface markings and firing, as well as the type of bonding used.

Points such as these have been discussed in previous chapters. When you view a house as a whole, a knowledge of the history of individual features helps you to place a building within a given period of time. The many combinations of features that make up a house seem numerous in the twentieth century, but are numerous as a result of an accumulation of styles over the centuries. At each period in the past, technology, social conditions and availability of materials dictated the appearance of the house. Homes in Southern England followed continental innovations more quickly than in the North.

It was easier to follow fashion where houses were timber-framed and rotted or burnt very readily, making sites available for change, than it was in regions where homes were built in sturdy stone.

Written evidence, in the form of house deeds for example, may establish the origins of a house, and even if the house is new, may reveal that the site has been built on several times in the past.

For general house studies, however, external features have to be the guide. Fortunately, there are styles of architecture typical of given periods that can be used, but

▲

105 Mixed styles in single houses. The nearest has an overhanging upper storey with timber posts and plastered walls, suggesting a seventeenth-century origin, but has been much restored. The second house has Victorian-styled gable dormers, but a Georgian pillared door and a solid chimney stack of a seventeenth-century period. Taking the oldest-looking features as a guide, these houses are probably of seventeenth-century origin.

106 A modernized late Victorian terrace. The nearest house is close to the appearance of the original style. The next house has very modern replacement windows and doors. The house on the left has Georgian-styled door and windows; in other words, the Victorian style has been replaced by older features.

▼

▲
107   A flint and thatch cottage — a reconstruction of a medieval style at the Weald and Downland Open Air Museum, near Chichester, Sussex.

common sense must be exercised and allowances made for the many "exceptions to the rule", and regional differences.

Medieval and Tudor Homes

This was the period of the timber-framed house and few examples of the earliest buildings exist. Examples of the cruck-framed house are now mainly found in Wales, the Midlands and Northern counties. In the South East the cruck frame was not popular and was soon replaced by the box frame method of construction and the Wealden House, for example, became a regional style. In the West Country cob or stone was favoured, as timber was never abundant.

When the Normans occupied Britain, the Saxons were building cruck-framed houses. The Saxons were originally a seafaring race and built wooden boats successfully, and they used this skill to build houses when they settled in England. The Normans, however, favoured building in stone wherever possible, and taught the Saxons their methods. The Saxon system of land ownership and jurisdiction was re-organized by the Normans after the conquest in 1066, although the village way of life remained. The Saxons were divided into three classes of men. The *freeholders* could sell or transfer their land, but paid for protection by the local lord of the manor. The *villeins*, who were the largest group, each farmed thirty strips in a common field, but were bound to work three days a week for the lord, without payment. And the *cottars* had only five strips of land, plus a cottage and garden, and only worked one day per week for the lord, so that they were free to hire themselves out as labourers for the rest of the week. After the Norman conquest the Saxons were much reduced in status; only one in eight were freemen, the rest were bound to their local lord, and only one lord of the manor out of a hundred was a Saxon. For two or three hundred years after the conquest, society had a marked Norman and Saxon culture. Large towns were granted charters, to free traders from the restrictions of their local lords, and began to expand.

In 1348 the Black Death destroyed half the population of Britain within two years. The plague spread quickly through the towns and in villages there were not enough people left to gather in the harvest. This disaster occurred just as the people were recovering from a freak change of climate that brought

◀ **108**   An early sixteenth-century manor house — another reconstruction at the Weald and Downland Open Air Museum. Note the jettied upper storey, widely spaced timbers with bracing, suggesting a shortage of timber in the area when built.

58

a period of very wet and cold years and ruined successive harvests.

In some areas the community was so reduced that villages were deserted. Their sites can still be seen today. In Lincolnshire, for example, grassy mounds in a field, around a ruined church tower, indicate the site of an abandoned village. The cottars, who could sell their labour on more days of the week than villeins, were sought after by the landlords, who paid them high wages. Because of the shortage of labour, sheep farming increased, as fewer men were needed to care for sheep than to cultivate crops. However, fields had to be fenced to control the sheep, and people disliked this enclosing of land that had been free before, for the peasants to graze their animals and gather firewood. Villeins became discontented and the social revolt in 1381, which led to one of their leaders, Wat Tyler, being put to death, started the breakdown of the bondage of peasants to landlords. Building during this period was limited.

The Tudor period was an era of progress for the English people, who were now integrated as a nation. The economy flourished with the increased production of wool and trade with Europe. Homes began to reflect the rising prosperity. Brick was more widely used by the people, at first for building chimney-stacks and for repairing wattle-and-daub infilling between posts of timber houses — *nogging* — and later in the period for building red brick houses. These were often built for the flourishing yeomen farmers and merchants, and had fine decorated chimneys, leaded lights in case-ment windows, and carved oak panelled rooms. The Tudor period was not without problems, however. The dissolution of the monasteries by Henry VIII in 1536 and 1539 led to more upheaval in society. A third of the land had been owned by the church and was now reallocated to landlords. The poor had used to rely on the charity of the monasteries to care for them in hard times, and now there was no one.

Elizabeth I brought stability to the economy, although wars still flourished and the poor and out-of-work filled the towns. The "four acre act", of 1588-89 said that no house was to be built within one mile of the sea, without four acres of land to go with it, so that the house owner might be able to grow food for the family. It was also hoped that this would stop speculative building in towns and put an end to the practice of peasants building on common land. It had been a tradition that if a house could be built on common land, between sundown and sunrise, i.e. in one night, and have walls, a roof and a fire burning in the hearth by dawn, then it should be allowed to remain.

Renaissance Building and Eighteenth-Century Homes

Travel abroad and the reading of books, which the printing presses (introduced in 1477 by William Caxton) were now pro-ducing, increased the awareness and know-ledge of the more influential people. New

109 This timber-framed sixteenth-century building in Horton Kirby, Kent has been well restored and brick nogging replaces the original wattle and daub.

▼

ideas about building houses began to be introduced — for example, by Inigo Jones (1573-1652), an architect who had travelled in Italy and studied the work of Andrea Palladio (1508-80). Palladio was an Italian architect, trained as a mason when young, but who had later studied and become interested in Greek and Roman classical architecture. He followed strict design rules for building and wrote *Four Books of Architecture*, which were published in 1570. Inigo Jones acquired copies of the books and began using the ideas to build homes in England. Symmetry and balance of features were the main theme of the Palladian style.

Late Tudor and Jacobean houses first show the new trends of Renaissance building — hipped roofs giving a flattened roof line, chimneys on outer end walls, parapets screening the roof and symmetrically placed windows. The late Tudor houses still had dripstones, but these were discontinued with the introduction of sash windows. Christopher Wren (1632-1723) followed Inigo Jones's lead, but adapted the Palladian style in rebuilding London after the Great Fire of 1666. The plans for rebuilding London were backed by legislation, but not all the plans were put into practice. However, the idea of town planning had been introduced and terraced housing appeared.

By the end of the seventeenth century brick was still a fashionable building material for walls, but quoins in raised blocks of brick or white stone — often Portland — emphasized the rectangular shape of the building. Panelled front doors, enhanced by canopies and pediments and flanked by pillars, were typical of the Queen Anne style of a rich man's house. Poor people's homes were not immediately affected by Renaissance architecture, but were gradually influenced by new building materials and building techniques. Large sash windows, typically three panes of glass wide by four or six high, were inappropriate for small houses, so that casement windows or the Yorkshire sliding sash were used.

The eighteenth-century homes reflected a prosperous, stable society and one that indulged in the classic architectural styles. Stone was the fashionable wall building material, and so cheaper, though unfashionable, brick walls were plastered — *stuccoed* — to give the effect of stone walls.

In the early part of the century there was a growth in cottage industry, especially when the exporting of raw wool was forbidden. Weaving was done by the family in their home, and houses had extra windows put into upstairs rooms, to give more light to looms. The production of woollen cloth increased with the invention of the "fly shuttle" by John Kay in 1733. Large looms could now be worked by one person instead of two. The need to provide more yarn for the weavers led to the invention of the Spinning Jenny in 1764 by James Hargreaves. The discovery of a method of smelting iron with coal and the introduction of the steam engine by James Watt in 1769 heralded the Industrial Revolution. By the end of the eighteenth century the cottage industries had moved, reluctantly, into factories. Cotton and woollen mills were built in Lancashire and Yorkshire.

110   Chiswick House, London (1726-36), is a good example of the Palladian style. Notice the symmetry of design, flattened hipped roof, ashlar block walls — all features which were adapted for smaller fashionable homes.

▼

On the farms, agricultural methods were also improved, and *crop rotation* was introduced, which increased the fertility of the soil and reduced pest concentrations. In a four-year cycle, a field may grow barley the first year, then a root crop such as turnips, a third year wheat and the fourth year clover. Clover roots produce nitrogen, which fertilizes the soil and the plant is fed to sheep and cattle. Turnips are stored as an animal winter feed and so larger herds and flocks were kept until spring. (Nowadays crop rotation is not strictly followed as chemical fertilizers and pesticides are widely used.) Cattle and sheep were now being fed root vegetables in winter and larger herds and flocks produced more meat. Land had been enclosed gradually for centuries, but now most of the common and waste land was finally hedged in. Food supplies increased five-fold, but country people, displaced by new farming methods, were seeking work in the new factories.

Town housing was a priority need and builders bought up land and laid out terraces in rows, along avenues, around squares or gardens and crescents. Architects became famous for their work. For example, John Nash (1752-1835) and Robert Adam (1728-92) built beautifully symmetrical terraces in London, and in Bath. The architect, John Wood, built Bath's Royal Crescent in 1769. Terraced homes were built for both rich and poor families. A better home would be a four-storey terrace house with a ground floor partly below street level and a basement. The first floor would be used for the principal living rooms. Sash windows, panelled front doors with fanlight, and a short flight of steps leading to the door were typical. The grey slate roof became popular and was concealed by a parapet or balustrade. Poorer homes were in terraces of identical brick two-storey houses, two-up, two-down style, and many were back-to-back, allowing no through-ventilation. Georgian shop fronts were made distinctive by bowed or barrel-shaped windows.

▲

111 A Queen Anne house in Stepney, London. The canopied door and rounded glass fanlight are typical features, together with the sash windows, parapeted eave to the hipped roof, and imposing pediment in the centre of the frontage.

Nineteenth-Century Homes

At the beginning of the nineteenth century, the Regency period, architects continued the classic style of building so popular over the past one hundred years. Brick-built houses, plastered with stucco and painted to imitate stone, flourished, with fine wrought-iron

112 Seventeenth-century houses. Variable window heights, sizes and styles, together with plastered walls with little recessing of the doors and windows, suggest timber-framed buildings.

▼

113   A Georgian terrace in Bedford Square, London, built in 1780. This is typical town housing of the period. Notice the basements, spider-web fanlights over emphasized doors and parapeted, low-pitched roof.

114   The Peabody Estate, Covent Garden, London, built in 1881 — solid, austere brick building, with sash windows and banks of chimneys on the roof. These were functional flats for cheap-rent homes.

balconies and railings, curved bay windows and round-topped doors. These were typical of the better homes. The houses for poor people in towns deteriorated, and elegant Georgian terraces were converted into flats, which soon became slums. Some land-owners became aware of the deplorable housing conditions of the poor and experimented by building model villages, housing estates, flats and tenements in towns. For example, an American merchant living in London, George Peabody, helped finance the building of five- and six-storey tenement blocks for the poor. Slum clearance began in London when Trafalgar Square was built and Nelson's Column was erected in 1843, on land known as Porridge Island, which had been cleared of delapidated buildings. An organization which preceded the London County Council of 1888, called the Metropolitan Board of Works, was set up in 1855 and made great changes by clearing slums, putting in main drains and establishing parks. During this early part of the Victorian period house styles were changing to the ornate Gothic style, and brick in different colours was in fashion. Later, a variety of styles were seen, as the Victorians sought something different and more impressive. The typical Victorian villa type of home was built in the suburbs and had a slate roof, a chimney-pot for each room in the house with a fireplace — which was most of them, brick walls in patterns, and sash windows of two by two panes, in rectangular or rounded bays that were decorated with pillars. Lintels were ornamented with moulded bricks, and a third of the front door was made of glass panels. The front doors also had black cast-iron door furnishings and were recessed into the house to make a porch. A tiled path led to the door through a small front garden. Also typical in poor areas were unending rows of similar-styled terraced houses, with slate roofs, many chimney-pots and no front garden. Cellars and attics were popular too.

In 1890 the Housing of the Working Classes Act supported slum clearance and

115 A Victorian house in Hampstead, London. Note the two-tone brick colouring, the ornate brickwork on the chimney-stack and gable, which is surmounted by a figure, and the pedimented, arched doorway.

116 A Victorian villa, Hampstead, 1890 – a typical suburban home, with characteristic door and porch, tiled front path, and sashed bay windows. Notice the firebreak wall on the roof.

provided loans to local authorities to promote house building. The back-to-back terraces were a major target for clearance or improvement by the turn of the century.

Better homes for the factory workers was another theme in housing development at this time. Rich businessmen had complete communities built for their work force, including shops, schools and churches, besides well-built homes with gardens. Sir Titus Salt built Saltaire near Bradford in Yorkshire in 1871. In 1886 Port Sunlight was built by Lever Brothers, and Bournville near Birmingham was completed in 1895 by Cadburys. Sir Joseph Rowntree added Earswick near York to the list of model housing estates in 1905.

Twentieth-Century Homes

The concern for building better urban environments for ordinary people led to the

117 Model workers' cottages adjacent to Abbey Mills Pumping Station, Bow, London. Note the church-style gothic windows and prominent chimney-stacks with varying pots. The roofs are slate and the walls in two-tone brick.

Garden City developments. Letchworth (1904), Hampstead Garden suburb, opened in 1907, and Welwyn Garden City, started in 1920, are examples of such towns. Public transport by rail, and later by road, caused towns to spread into the country-side. Semi-detached houses lined major roads between towns, in what was termed "ribbon development". Houses were built to rent by local councils and for sale by private developers.

By the start of the Second World War in 1939, the three bedroomed semi-detached house was popular — brick-built, with pebble-dashed walls, bay windows in the front room, french windows at the back of the house, kitchen and bathroom included, but cellar and attic absent. Terraces were still the historic two-up, two-down, but a bathroom and toilet were now provided. The bungalow also became popular at this time — a modern version of the single-storey house that had always been popular in rural areas.

Home comforts and labour-saving devices were increasing. Gas and electricity were installed in most urban homes, for use in cooking and lighting, but coal and coke were still the heating fuels. Domestic appliances, such as vacuum cleaners, electric irons and radios, began to appear in ordinary homes before the war, but it was not until the 1950s that most home owners could afford washing machines, refrigerators and television sets.

Coal fires were being superseded by central heating. Oil- and gas-fired heaters produced hot water to circulate through pipes to radiators. Electric central heating was also introduced widely by the 1970s.

Post-war planners of new housing did not realize how soon the motor car would be in use by so many people, and garages were not included in early post-war council-built or privately-built houses. This has led to congested roads in older areas of towns, due to

◀ 118 Pebble-dashed, three-bedroomed, semi-detached house built in 1936. Note that there is no garage space and the large casement windows in timber frames.

street parking. Modern houses often have the garage built into the main structure of the house or adjacent to it.

High-rise blocks of flats were seen as the answer to the housing shortages of the cities. But these have since become unpopular. Structural faults and the isolation which people living in them feel, together with problems with children's playing facilities for example, have now made low-rise blocks of flats and town houses, with two upper floors and an integral garage, the modern trend in town building.

Modern houses have large panes of glass in their windows — picture-frame type — front doors of decorative glass, and plastic gutters. Walls are still of brick, but in stretcher bond, indicating cavity walls. Roofs are of cement tiles, often in subtle colours, and chimney-pots are reduced to a single flue for gas- or oil-fired central heating systems or no chimney at all in the "all-electric home".

Houses of the future will, no doubt, reflect the pending shortages and high cost of fuel. Home insulation will become a priority, and windows will not use such large panes of glass and will be of double thickness. Doors, too, will be double-glazed. Plastics will continue to be used for gutters and piping, as metal prices increase. Brick and concrete should still be economic materials for walls; stone will always be expensive. Regional styles and materials, no doubt, will persist, but there will be a national building style for most houses, as building materials and pre-fabricated parts will be easily transported by modern travel methods.

Although the appearance of houses has changed during the past one thousand years, the modern home is still the centre of family life. It provides, as it has done in the past, shelter from the climate, security for the family themselves and their possessions, and a base from which to seek a living, to return to and relax in.

▲
119   A bungalow built in Epping, Essex, in 1928. The roof tiles are glazed in a pantile style which was popular at this time, especially in seaside towns.

120   A modern house in Mill Hill, London, built ▶ in 1977. Notice the all-glass front door, no chimneys, but roof vents on the ridge.

9
Over to You

Look at Houses

Initially, the best thing to do if you have become interested in houses is to go and look at them. Look at your own home, those in your street, village or town. Obtain an Ordnance Survey map of your area and it might tell you more about it. Look for similarities and differences between houses. You may become attracted to certain features of houses, and take a particular interest, for example, in doors, chimneys or windows.

Recording

The need to record what you see may now become important. Whether you specialize in a feature, whole houses or an area, the different aspects may be photographed or sketched on site and then drawn or painted carefully later. Postcards and pictures from magazines can also be collected to illustrate your theme. A large loose-leafed scrap book is probably the simplest way to store your pictures and notes. All pictures should have notes made about them, the date when seen, the address of the site, and the building materials used, plus all you can discover about the site. This information may become historically important in later years,

especially if the building is demolished or altered. Black and white pictures should also include notes about the colours of the building, as colours change with fashion and may be of interest later. Card index systems are also a useful way of recording your features. A limited project may be recorded in tapestry or embroidery — your house, for example.

Three-dimensional records can also be made, perhaps as attractive clay models, or wood carvings. Card can be used to make a village or street scene. Three-dimensional model villages can be seen in many parts of the country, especially at seaside resorts, and they make an intriguing place to visit, where further ideas may be gathered.

History

To find out more about the history of your house, village or town, you may need to research into written documents. The deeds of your house may make interesting reading and a visit to the local reference library will prove invaluable. The County Architects department at the local council office may also advise you about local maps, scheduled buildings and future development schemes. The county archives will bring you into contact with original documents, if you wish to find out details of the past, and you may be able to obtain photocopies of some documents.

Recent local history can be discovered by talking to older residents of the area. If the houses you are interested in are on a new estate, find out what the land was used for before the houses came. Local people may have stories to tell of the area and photographs to show you. If a site is being prepared for new buildings, photograph the site before, during and after construction. Add all the details you can gather to your records, on the materials used, building methods, time taken, local newspaper references, and occupiers. The many everyday facts recorded about the new building will become fascinating reading in fifty years' time and may be the only detailed record left for future local historians!

Materials

If building materials interest you, a look at the local geology will be worthwhile. Where the local houses are made of stone, find out what kind it is and where it came from. If the house is old, the quarry may not be far away, perhaps still as a quarry or revealed in the name of a street or area. Take care and ask permission first before visiting quarries; they can be dangerous. Make your own museum of building materials. Collect old and new examples of such things as bricks, tiles, chimney-pots, gutters and door furnishings. Label all your exhibits with everything you know about them. Talk to a friendly builder's merchant about the stock he "carries". There are many different types of bricks made today, each with a name and specific use. Even the sand he sells will be of different kinds and come from many places. He may also sell chimney-pots and slates. Old building materials may be found on demolition sites, but you must ask the site foreman before removing any material or entering the site — it might be dangerous.

Timber yards are also fascinating places to visit and the tangy scent of the wood resins adds another dimension to this material. Timber is imported from many countries and the timber merchant may tell you about the different woods and plywoods he stocks.

In some towns glazier's merchants can be found and the variety of different types of glass now manufactured is amazing. You may be able to make a collection from off-cuts, but care and thought about how to keep such a collection will be needed.

Talking to a builder, perhaps a family friend, will also be very worthwhile. The traditional names given by the builder to his tools and materials make valuable social history and should be recorded. These names could vary in different parts of the country.

Visits

It will be of mutual benefit if you first enquire by telephone or letter, when seeking information from any one, to ask if they are willing to help you. Arrange to visit the person when he is not too busy and for a set time. Have your questions ready and take down the answers on a tape recorder if possible, or make full notes. If your questions are rather complex, give a list to the person before the meeting so that answers may be looked up. People will usually talk about their work if a sensible approach is made and a sincere interest is shown in their subject. A "thankyou" is the least you can give in return for first-hand information not readily available in books!

There are many societies throughout the country interested in the local environment, which may be of help and interest to you. Local history societies, conservation groups and village societies, for example, will all usually be listed at the local library and may be worth joining.

If you wish to visit places where ordinary homes can be seen, a local tourist office, the National Tourist Board or, again, the local library will be able to tell you where and when such places are open. For example, some towns are famous for their historic buildings, such as Chester and York for timber-framed houses, Bath for eighteenth-century terraces, or Milton Abbes in Dorset for thatched cottages. Many counties have open air museums where you can walk into homes of the past. The following are good examples:

The North of England Open Air Museum, Beamish Hall, Stanley, C. Durham.
The Weald and Downland Open Air Museum, Singleton, Nr. Chichester, Sussex.
Abbeydale Industrial Hamlet, Sheffield.
Kirkstall Abbey Museum, West Yorkshire.
The Welsh Folk Museum in Cardiff.

Model villages, are quite numerous, especially in seaside towns, and are worth visiting. They have often been built over a period of time, and already are historic records themselves, as changes occur annually in a town's landscape. For example, there is an extensive model town in Babbacombe, near Torquay, in Devon, and a model town of Wimborne, in Dorset. At Naseby, near Market Harborough, Northamptonshire, there is the Museum of Miniature Rural Buildings.

In conclusion, if you produce a scrap book or worthwhile record of houses that is factual and authentic, future local historians may appreciate it if you donate or lend it to the local library, when you wish your study to have a good home!

Organizations to Contact

British Tourist Authority,
64 St James' Street, London SW1A 1NF.

English Tourist Board,
4 Grosvenor Gardens, London SW1W 0DU.

Wales Tourist Board,
3 Castle Street, Cardiff CF1 2RE.

Scottish Tourist Board,
23 Ravelston Terrace, Edinburgh EH4 3EU.

The National Trust
Head Office: 42 Queen Anne's Gate, London SW1H 9AS.
Education Adviser: 8 Church Street, Lacock, Chippenham, Wiltshire SN15 2LB.

Local Public Libraries and Museums will have regional addresses for the above organizations and details of visiting times of local places of interest. Libraries and Museums will also have the names and addresses of Historical Societies and similar groups interested in the history and environment of your area. Local Planning Authorities may help you with maps of the district and aerial photographs. Suppliers of aerial photographs include:

Aerofilms Ltd,
Gate Studios, Station Road,
Boreham Wood, Herts WD6 1EJ.

Air Photographs Unit, Department of the Environment, Prince Consort House, Albert Embankment, London SE1 7TF.

The styles of features and materials used to build houses in different periods of history

Feature	Roman 400 AD	Saxon 1100 AD	Norman 12th Century	Middle Ages 13th-15th Century	Tudor 16th Century	Jacobean 17th Century	Georgian 18th Century	Victorian 19th Century	Modern 20th Century
Walls	Local stone; Wood, Wattle and daub with plaster; Thin brick	Cruck frame; Re-used Roman brick		Box frame; Flemish brick, Great English brick	Cob and plaster; Statute brick	Pargetting; Flemish bond	Weather board, Hung Tiles; Stucco rendering; Brick Tax 1784-1850	Cement; Improved brick production	Fletton and cement bricks; Pebbledash; Stretcherbond
Doors	Wood	Animal skin; Cloth	Solid wood; Metal pins		Wood door, wood frame; Flat hinge	Panelled door; "H" hinge	Door knockers; Glass panels; Fanlights; Concealed iron butt hinge	Letterboxes; Bells	All-glass door
Windows	Wind-holes; Roman glass	Oiled fabric, Paper, Horn; Shutters	Imported leaded lights	Gothic-style lancet windows	1579 windows made part of house; Leaded lights; Casement style; More glass (crown)	Wood frame; Fixed sash windows	Bow; Window Tax (1697-1851); Counter-balanced	Bay; Rolled glass	Picture; Metal frame; Double glazing; Float glass
Roof	Gable style; Pantiles, Thatch, Shingle, Stone slab			Some English clay tiles		Mansard; Pantiles; Dutch tiles; Dutch gable	Hipped; Slate; English tiles, clay	Nibs on tiles	Cement tiles
Chimneys	Flues in stone walls; Chimneys	Hole in roof; Louvre	A few chimneys	Fire hoods and reredos; Some pots; Pottery and wood louvres	Timber and mud stacks; Stone stacks; Carved brick	Increase in stacks, plastered; Late 17th century TAX	Brick stacks common; Handmade pots; Coal fires	Many moulded pots	Gas and oil flues or air vents; Few if any pots; Central heating

Only fairly wealthy people could afford new materials when first introduced. Poor homes remained simply constructed from local materials till the 18thC. Building styles overlap periods and features are renewed, so date carefully.

Books for Further Reading

Most suitable for ages 10-15

Gareth Adamson,
Machines at Home,
Puffin

L. G. Humphrys,
Glass and Glassmaking,
Basil Blackwell

Heinz Kurth,
Houses and Homes,
World's Work Ltd

Henry Pluckrose,
Houses,
Mills & Boon Ltd

Philip Sauvain,
Looking Around in Town and Country, Franklin Watts

T. A. Thompson,
The Story of Homes,
Basil Blackwell

R. J. Unstead,
Houses,
A. & C. Black Ltd

J. N. T. Vince,
Villages,
Basil Blackwell

Jan Williamson & Susan Meredith,
The Children's Book of Britain,
Usborne Publishing Ltd
(Contains a guide of places to visit)

Most suitable for ages 15-18

John Haddon,
Local Geography in Towns,
George Philip & Son

W. G. Hoskins,
Local History in England,
Longman

W. G. Hoskins,
Fieldwork in Local History,
Faber & Faber

Most suitable for age 18+

Henry Aaron,
Street Furniture Album,
Shire Publications

Sidney Oldall Addy,
The Evolution of the English House, E. P. Publishing Ltd

M. W. Barley,
The English Farmhouse and Cottage, Routledge & Kegan Paul

Alex Clifton-Taylor,
The Pattern of English Building,
Batsford

Pamela Cunningham,
How Old is your House?,
Alpha Books

Norman Davey,
History of Building Materials,
Phoenix House

Valentine Fletcher,
Chimney Pots and Stacks,
Centaur Press Ltd

John Penoyre & Michael Ryan,
The Observer's Book of Architecture,
Frederick Warne & Co Ltd

John Prizeman,
Your House — The Outside View,
Hutchinson

Marjorie and C. H. B. Quennell,
A History of Everyday Things in England, Batsford
(Five volumes covering different periods of British History)

J. R. Ravensdale,
History on Your Doorstep,
BBC 1982

Trudy West,
The Timber-framed House in England, David & Charles

Note
Books marked with an asterisk (*) can be found in libraries. Other books are available in libraries and from booksellers.

Index

The numbers in **bold type** refer to the figure numbers of the illustrations